VOCATION TO RE

Contemplation and ~~Change~~

❦

VOCATION
TO
RESISTANCE

Contemplation and Change

UNA KROLL

DARTON · LONGMAN + TODD

First published in 1995 by
Darton, Longman and Todd Ltd
1 Spencer Court
140–142 Wandsworth High Street
London SW18 4JJ

ISBN 0–232–52142–5

A catalogue record for this book is available from
the British Library

Unless otherwise stated scriptural quotations are from The New Jerusalem Bible
published and copyright 1985 by Darton, Longman and Todd Ltd
and Doubleday and Co Inc.

Design by Julia Lilauwala

Phototypeset in 11/13pt Bembo by Intype, London
Printed and bound in Great Britain
by Page Bros, Norwich

For Betty and Teresa
and all who gather
at the cross
to be
with
Jesus

CONTENTS

ᘓᑫᘔ

ACKNOWLEDGEMENTS

IN PREPARING this book I have had invaluable help from my friends Anne Czerniawska, Hazel Eyles, Betty Houghton, Teresa Pearson and Jane Tillier, who read early versions of the typescript and made constructive criticisms and comments.

I am grateful to the Revd James Coutts for generous access to his books and for a theological discussion which helped me to write Chapter 10.

Acknowledgements are due to the following for permission to quote copyright material: A. C. Black Ltd (Iulia de Beausobre: *Creative Suffering*); Georges Borchardt Inc. (Elie Wiesel: *Night*, © Les Editions de Minuit 1958, available from Penguin Books Ltd); Jonathan Cape (Alan Ereia: *The Heart of the World*); Darton, Longman and Todd Ltd (Constance Babington-Smith: *Iulia de Beausobre*; Robert Llewellyn (ed.) *Circles of Silence*; Charles Elliott: *Praying the Kingdom*; Metropolitan Anthony of Sourozh (Anthony Bloom): *School for Prayer*); J. M. Dent Ltd (Nicholas de Cusa: *The Vision of God*, tr. Emma Gurney Salter); Editions du Seuil (Teilhard de Chardin: *Hymn of the Universe*); Faber & Faber Ltd (Dag Hammarskjöld: *Markings*); Farrar, Strauss & Giroux Ltd (Isaac Bashevis Singer: *Stories for Children*); Hodder & Stoughton Ltd (Margaret Duggan (ed): *Through the Year with Michael Ramsey*); Penguin Books Ltd (Fyodor Dostoyevsky: *The Brothers Karamazov*); St Paul's Press (Cardinal Basil Hume: *To Be a Pilgrim*); SCM Ltd (Paul Tournier: *The Violence Inside*); Sheldon Press (Thomas Merton: *Conjectures of a Guilty Bystander*); SPCK (John Polkinghorne: *One World*); A. P. Watt Ltd on behalf of J. W. Prestcott and Mrs S. C. Thedinga (H. F. M. Prestcott: *The Man on a Donkey*).

The publisher would be glad to hear from any copyright holder whom they have been unable to trace. Due acknowledgement will be made in future editions of this book.

So stand your ground,
with truth a belt round your waist,
and uprightness a breastplate,
wearing for shoes on your feet
the eagerness to spread the gospel of peace
and always carrying the shield of faith
so that you can use it to quench
the burning arrows of the Evil One.
And then you must take
salvation as your helmet
and the sword of the Spirit,
that is, the word of God. (Eph. 6: 14–17)

Introduction

∞✞∞

Pray and Stand Firm

The people who know their God will stand firm
and take action (Dan. 11: 33)

No one need search for a programme of action
or a crusade. The world and suffering humanity
create the agenda for those who have eyes for
human misery, ears for the stories of oppression
and degradation and hearts to respond to the
distress of our human family. (Basil Hume OSB)[1]

PASSIONATE FEELINGS underlie this book. They come
from listening to the stories of people all over the world.
They come from a heart sensitised to misery through prayer.
They come from an enduring thirst to see changes in our
world, changes that will bring us all just a little closer to the
day when the Kingdom of God will come. I find this degree
of passion difficult to understand. It should have been worn
down by repeated disappointments, growing older, becoming
more realistic than I was when I was a young idealist. It has
not been. I remain as thirsty to see God's will done on earth
as I was when I was first converted at the age of eighteen.

My life has taken me into all sorts of places and situations. I
have been something of a polymath: this has meant that I have
accumulated many different roles on my journey through life.
Yet it is true to say that there has only been one vocation, the
call to follow Jesus wherever he goes. Throughout my life there
have been times when I have pleaded with God to stop calling
me to new ways of prayer, new adventures, new tasks, new
roles. Yet when the calls come, I follow because there is no
other response that seems possible. This kind of single-

1

mindedness can only be attributed to the grace of God. It certainly isn't natural to me.

I remain convinced that being a Christian is the most satisfying form of life on earth. It seems to me that my task in writing this book is to express some of that delight, some of that thirst for God that keeps me praying, some of that zeal for the Kingdom that has impelled me into pastoral, political and social action, that has made me heed those words of Daniel 'The people who know their God will stand firm and take action' (Dan. 11: 33), and those even stronger words of St Paul: 'So stand your ground, with truth a belt round your waist, and uprightness a breastplate, wearing for shoes on your feet the eagerness to spread the gospel of peace, and always carrying the shield of faith so that you can use it to quench the burning arrows of the Evil One' (Eph. 6: 14–17).

This introduction has a twofold purpose. In sharing part of my own journey, I hope to show how much Christian attitudes towards a life of prayer have changed during the past fifty years. In sharing some of my own experience of the call to 'stand firm', I hope to point to the necessary links between prayer, witness and action in a world in which Christians are called to 'pray constantly' (1 Thess. 5: 17).

On the Call to 'Pray Constantly'

When I was young, it was common to find people who thought that continuous contemplative prayer[2] was the proper work of a select group of people who were 'experts'. Now, on the other hand, there is a more widespread recognition that a contemplative disposition[3] is a gift that is given by God to many different types of people. God can, and does, invite anyone, anywhere, under any circumstance to contemplate and to pray 'at all times and in all places'.[4] Many people today do not join religious orders. Instead, they look to other contemplatives living in the world for their support and nourishment, either through 'base communities',[5] or through various forms of network. That didn't happen very often fifty years ago. It certainly didn't happen to me. When I was a newly qualified doctor I was pointed towards a religious order in which prayer and mission had an equal part. I duly went off and joined it.

I stayed five years, but then felt called back to medicine. I left the order, married, became a mother and worked, first as a missionary doctor in Africa, then as a general medical practitioner in England. When my husband died in 1987, our four children had grown to maturity and were pursuing independent lives. I felt a strong call to explore what it meant to be a widow in the New Testament style. I was of the right age, and I had fulfilled the conditions set out in the first letter to Timothy, an early Church leader (1 Tim. 5: 9–10). I thought I would see what it meant to be someone who 'left on her own has set her hope on God and perseveres night and day in petitions and prayer' (1 Tim. 5: 5).

I couldn't quite picture living like Judith, daughter of Merari, widow of Manasseh. She

> stayed inside her home for three years and four months. She had an upper room built for herself on the roof. She wore sackcloth next to the skin and dressed in widow's weeds. She fasted every day of her widowhood except for the Sabbath eve, the Sabbath itself, the eve of New Moon, the feast of New Moon and the joyful festivals of the House of Israel. (Judith 8: 4–7)

Besides, Judith had been called out to deliver her people:

> when she had finished praying . . . she removed the sackcloth she was wearing and taking off her widow's dress she washed all over, anointed herself plentifully with perfumes, dressed her hair, wrapped a turban round it and put on the robe of joy she used to wear when her husband Manasseh was still alive. She put sandals on her feet, put on her necklaces, bracelets, rings, earrings and all her jewellery, and made herself beautiful enough to beguile the eye of any man who saw her. (Judith 10: 1–4)

Then she sallied forth to seduce Holofernes and to kill him by beheading him with a scimitar (Judith 13). After that she went back to being a widow (Judith 16: 22).

Being a confirmed pacifist, unable to kill flies, let alone

people, I knew this kind of heroic witness wasn't for me. I thought, however, that I might manage to emulate the prophetess Anna, the daughter of Phanuel, 'who never left the temple, serving God night and day with fasting and prayer' (Luke 2: 36–8). As far as I could see at the time, knowing what I did then, that meant finding a religious community whose vocation matched that aim to help me to pray in that way. I already knew a small community of contemplative nuns in Wales, the Society of the Sacred Cross. I hoped that their convent, Tymawr, might become my 'temple'. Being traditional enough to think that the sisters would teach me how to pray continually, I went to them and eventually joined the Society. I shall always be grateful for what I learnt during my six years with the nuns.

In the end, however, the Spirit drove me out. The reasons for leaving were complex, but a primary reason was my conviction that God, who had asked me 'to leave the world', was now asking me to return to it to 'build a cell of quiet', and to pray there. The implication was that if this was a call of God I would need to live alone.

Initially, I found this idea startling. I had never lived alone, having spent all my life in a family or community. For six years I had treasured the benefits of living in a religious community, where one had the support of the religious vows, regular times for prayer, protection from outside intrusion and the companionship of other people who were also trying to live lives of prayer. So when I heard this small nagging 'voice' inside me, and had to think about the practical problems of living a life of continuous prayer outside the 'temple gates', I felt quite alarmed.

As a professed nun, I had no intention of abandoning my vows, nor was I at all eager to leave my community. Nevertheless, the small voice kept on insisting that I thought about trying to live a solitary form of monastic life in a rather unusual way. There were many barriers to surmount, not least those within my own personality.

My own preconceptions of the solitary life, compounded by the traditions of recent monastic practice, were a hindrance to me. The traditions of the religious life during the past five hundred years suggested that a monk or nun who wanted to live a solitary life of any sort had to undergo quite a long period of formation in a monastic community before testing their vocation to solitude. Those who were discontented with community life need not apply for such permission. Only those who were of proven worth and stability could expect to be allowed to try such an eccentric form of religious life. If you wanted to live a life of prayer alone you had to go into a community first, learn the basic principles of the religious life and then wait until the community agreed that you should adopt the solitary way of life. Several people I knew had done that, among them Father William of Glasshampton, Father Whittemore of the Order of the Holy Cross, and Brother Ramon of the Society of St Francis. My contact with such people through their writings and books I had read about them inspired considerable awe.[6] Solitaries were generally thought to be 'holy' people, called into lives of heroic love for all humankind, called to live alone, yet freed to be companion to everyone in the world, called to seek God's face through continuous prayer and fasting.

These initial preconceptions may have been quite false, but when I first thought about becoming a kind of hermit,[7] I had no chance of finding out. At that time, I thought that hermits did not see other people: they only talked rarely to a few special souls. I was unlikely to be one of those chosen people. However, during my years of convent life I became handmaid to a hermit for a time. I also met and talked with a couple of other hermits. Some of my false ideas went out of the window, but I still thought of them as rather special people. I warmed to the ones who lived in the town, at the top of high-rise flats, in run-down areas of inner cities. One of my fellow-novices went off to live in a church tower in a large city. I thought that was wonderful, but I knew I couldn't live like that.

The only way to find out how I could follow Jesus in the way that he, rather than I, wanted was to risk everything and start living alone. With the consent of my sisters, I set out on a trial year. I went to live in a small house set within the parish churchyard of a country town close to the border between Wales and England.

During that first year I met various people who were already living the kind of life I wanted to explore. Some of these people had begun their lives of prayer in established religious communities. Then, often after years of faithful observance of the Rule and customs of their order, they had left with or without the support of their parent community. Now some were hermits, some were anchorites,[8] some lay contemplatives,[9] living quietly in the world. Most of them were living alone, but a few had arranged to live in the same house or close to each other so that they could sometimes meet for worship and mutual support. As I listened to some of their stories I felt a great affinity with many of them. I discovered what it was that united me to them and to other people who lived lives of prayer outside monasteries and convents. It was a thirst for and a capacity for interior solitude.

This thirst for solitude, for times of prayer when one can be alone with God, is, I believe, a primary condition for those who are called to a life of prayer and witness in the world. This does not mean that we are necessarily called to live alone or to be alone for substantial periods of time. It simply means that we are drawn into solitude to commune with God. One can be alone with God in this way anywhere and at any time, even in the middle of an outwardly busy life.

As potential witnesses to Kingdom values[10] we have to be so rooted in God that we can survive the storms and tidal waves of evil that will inevitably break over our heads when we try to witness to the primacy of Christ in our lives. It is rather like being a plant with a taproot. The root grows deep into the soil to find water. When it does the growing point of the plant can thrust itself through the earth and flourish. So it is with us: only if we are deeply rooted in God can we grow and bear fruit in God's Kingdom.

Still clinging to my own religious community, I thrust my roots deep into solitude, into God, and found them entwined with those of many other people who had never seen inside a convent or monastery. These were people who had undertaken the task of living lives of prayer in the world without first going into a monastery or convent for training. They were learning as they went along.

There were a variety of people living in this way. Their

numbers seemed to be growing. Some were single, others married. Many of these people did not recite any formal Office, nor did they necessarily depend on the Eucharist to the same extent as I had formerly done. Some of them did not spend a great deal of time in formal personal prayer, and yet they were splendid witnesses for Christ. They stood firmly against evil. They showed Christ's face to the world by the quality of their loving care for others. They were people who were at peace with God, themselves and others, and they radiated that peace wherever they went.

These meetings with very ordinary people, inconspicuous, gentle, loving people, who were so steeped in God that they were effective witnesses to Kingdom values, influenced my life. They changed the way I thought about a life of prayer, the way I lived alone, the way I was at last able to let go of all my religious community anchors for the sake of doing what I thought God wanted me to do. At the end of my probationary year I asked to be released from my obligations to the Society of the Sacred Cross and was granted that release six months later.

I still live alone in that small house. I now live under vows and a way of life approved and protected by my diocesan bishop. I do some work for the parish as its deacon. I spend a fair amount of each day in prayer; I can also offer warm and homely hospitality to anyone who seeks a quiet place in which to pray, read, think and rest.

For more than fifty years now I have been reflecting on what it means to be a Christian in relationship to God, God's creation, and my companions who are human beings. The search for answers to my restless questioning can neither be found in myself nor in other people, but only, as St Augustine teaches us, in God.

I was eighteen years old when I first opened Augustine's *Confessions* and began to read the first chapter, in which he writes: 'Thou hast created us for thyself, and our heart cannot be quieted till it may find repose in thee.'[11] What struck me then, and still does, is that he did not say 'thou hast created *me*' but 'thou hast created *us*'. He did not say '*my* heart cannot be quieted' but '*our* heart cannot be quieted'. He suggests that all human beings are bound up with each other and can only find their individual happiness when all have found 'repose' in God. My own sense of belonging to a community of faith began with those words and is undiminished now that I am 'old and grey-haired' (Ps. 71: 18). It was because I became conscious of not being an individual standing alone before God, but a member of the Body of Christ, that I joined a Christian Church and found myself belonging to a praying community.

Although I had been baptised as an infant and had prayed to something, or someone, inside and outside myself ever since I could remember, it was only when I made a conscious decision to commit my life to the search for that 'repose' in God of which St Augustine speaks that I began to discover other people going in the same direction, being on the same quest.

It was because I needed to learn to pray that I began to go to church. When I first became a Christian I thought that everyone was going in the same direction in the same way, but that was because I happened to join a local Church that encouraged its members to worship in a particular way. It wasn't long before I discovered that God makes use of people's temperaments, preferences and gifts in all sorts of different ways so that, although people seek God in distinctive ways, they will in the end meet in God. Increasingly, as I have grown older, my own life has been greatly enriched through having experienced a variety of ways of worshipping God both corporately and individually. Although I have my own preferences, these do not cause me to deny the validity of other people's religious practices and customs, but rather to respect them and learn from them.

This book will be concerned mainly with personal prayer and so I need to define what I mean when I use that term. For me, prayer is a relationship with God, initiated by God to help us to become aware of God's presence and activity in the world.[12]

Prayer is initiated by God, yet because God never forces us into a relationship, we are always invited to play our part in this convenant relationship. Our part in prayer consists in learning to wait upon God, waiting to become aware of the Holy Spirit who prays in us and of Christ who takes us to the Father, in whom 'we live, and move, and exist' (Acts 17: 28). As we grow into that awareness of God's presence in and around us we realise that prayer is God's continual activity in us.

Through prayer we become aware of God's desire for creation, for us and for all humankind. Consequently we stop thinking of prayer as a recurrent activity that we indulge in from time to time when we feel like it, or have the opportunity. We begin to see that the Holy Spirit is always turning us towards God, always inviting us to overhear what is being said among the three persons of the Trinity, always inviting us to join in their dance of Love. We begin to join in.

There are as many ways of joining in the dance of Love as there are people in God's family. All ways of prayer are equally valid. The old man who sits in church and gazes at God becomes attuned to God's presence with him. Monks and nuns chanting their Offices seven times a day, and rising by night to keep watch with Christ, become familiar with God's words and attributes. The contemplative cloistered nun, or monk, beating upon the 'cloud of unknowing', searches for Love in the darkness.[13] The devout Christian who breathes the Jesus prayer[14] all day long finds God's presence woven into her or his daily life; so too does the housewife, peeling the potatoes while she chatters to God; so too do the busy professionals who make arrow prayers to God at intervals through the day, knowing that God will remember them even if they forget God. The missionary, near or far from home, struggling to survive in an alien culture, finds God at the heart of it. The charismatic who prays in tongues, or uses God's gifts in other ways, feels and is close to the source of all creative energy; so too are the people who are touched by God at crisis points in their lives, and who never forget that fact but go 'in the strength of that meat forty days and forty nights' (1 Kgs. 19: 8), or even all the days of their lives. The dying, gasping the only prayer they remember from childhood, are held in God's love as they are born into their new life.

God loves us so much that even if we do stray, consciously refuse the relationship God offers us, and flirt with sin or make sin our bedfellow, we still may find Love waiting for us round the next corner, as St Paul did on the road to Damascus (Acts

9). Even if we deny God's existence we may be suddenly overwhelmed by an encounter with God.

Sudden and unexpected encounters with God are never forgotten. They become points of reference, moments of sustenance, acknowledged turning points in one's life. Nevertheless, the insights that they bring need to be nurtured and brought to fulfilment by a life of fidelity to gospel values. Otherwise the moment of contact with God becomes a moment to be remembered but not a moment of turning, a moment of transformation by God.[15]

Most of us, however, do not become aware of God's abiding presence suddenly. Worship and personal prayer bring moments of awareness. These become more frequent and then habitual as we explore our relationship with God. We may lose our sense of God for periods of time, but often it returns for long enough to sustain us through the next period of aridity and darkness. There are, I believe, some people who have to walk their whole journey by faith alone. They know by faith that God is always with them, but they are not aware of his abiding presence. They have to deduce it at an intellectual level by what they see happening around them. Nevertheless, they are still held within God's dance of Love.

In all these circumstances our task in the covenant relationship with God is to be faithful and to develop our attentiveness towards God through regular worship and prayer. As we undertake this task we will need to find ways of praying that help us to become more attuned to what God is doing in us, in others and in all creation.

It is not my task in this book to discuss all the various ways of learning to pray that are available to Christians who are serious about their faith. There are many good books and manuals about prayer that are available to those who want to explore techniques of prayer, and some of these are listed in the Select Bibliography. All that I am suggesting here is that those who take their relationship with God seriously enough to want to become aware of what God is doing in their lives, in other people's lives and in the whole of creation will find themselves taken into the heart of God; in that heart they will find the whole universe.

When God touches our lives, when we are drawn into the heart of the Blessed Trinity, we will find that we cannot dance this dance of Love as a stately recreational minuet, a pleasant private act, a personal enjoyment that others do not share, a narcissistic act of sensual delight. As we follow God we shall find that Love takes us out into the world to see what God is already doing there.

As we come to abide in God, we begin to see creation and our fellow creatures with the eyes of God. We begin to be moved by compassion and concern in new ways. We discover what God is asking us to do, so that others too may be encouraged to join in that exchange of Love. It will not necessarily mean that we will engage in political or social action in the world. But it does always mean that as Christian disciples we have a purpose that will become apparent to others by the way in which we live our lives to the praise and glory of God, for, as St Paul reminded the Christians at Ephesus:

> now you too, in him, have heard the message of the truth and the gospel of your salvation, and having put your trust in it you have been stamped with the seal of the Holy Spirit of the Promise, who is the pledge of our inheritance, for the freedom of the people whom God has taken for his own, for the praise of his glory. (Eph. 1: 17–18)

On the Call to Stand Firm

This book is about what happens to some of us when we are invited to join in God's dance of Love. It is my experience that contact with the Source of all love and life can, and often does, change us to such an extent that our behaviour towards other people and towards the whole of God's creation also alters. One way in which we may be changed by God is through receiving a call to live lives of constant prayer 'in the world, yet not of it' (cf. John 17: 14–23). This book is about that call and some of the various ways in which it may be lived out to the praise and glory of God through prayer and learning to stand firmly against evil.

It is my belief, a belief that is supported by contact with

other Christian disciples, that in our Western world at this time in history, towards the end of the second millennium, God is asking many Christians to learn to 'pray constantly' (1 Thess. 5: 17) right at the heart of the world in and through the ordinary circumstances of their lives.

This call is coming to all sorts of people. It is coming to married people, to people living in partnerships or in small groups of one kind or another. It is coming to people who are living alone. It summons people from all denominations. It is coming to people who are gregarious by nature and to those who are drawn to solitude. It attracts men and women. The call comes to busy people in full employment and to housewives with so much to do that they can hardly fit everything into one day. It comes to unemployed people with too much time on their hands. God is calling retired people to rethink their lifestyle. God is calling those who are rejects in society, the sick, aged, infirm, housebound, those who are confined to a wheelchair or are bedbound.

I have often wondered why this call is coming to so many people at this time. One important reason may be that Christianity in the Western world is again in the same kind of missionary situation that existed in the first few centuries after Christ's death. In the early years of Christianity the evils of pagan society were challenged by the faith and lifestyles of Christians. Many of them were persecuted and martyred for the faith. By the fourth and fifth centuries, however, Christianity had become part of the structure of society. There were many signs that moral and social evils had established themselves in the Christian Church itself as well as in the prevailing culture of society. Some Christians saw the dangers and addressed the evils by sound doctrinal, moral and spiritual teaching. At the same time thousands of ardent Christians went out of the cities and into the deserts to devote their lives to prayer and thus fight the evils that had accrued in post-Constantinian Western Christian society.[16]

In our own generation the Western Christian Churches are struggling to witness to the faith in a hostile environment. In many countries the prevailing spiritual and moral climate seems to be post-Christian. Moreover, many younger people in West-

ern society have only the vaguest knowledge of the central
tenets of the Christian faith. Even when they do know the
basic stories about the life of Christ, many do not see any
relevance in them to the way in which they actually live their
lives. Christians themselves are often bewildered by current
theological discussions within the Church. Many struggle with
doctrines that are central to the faith: some have apparently
ceased to believe in resurrection life.[17] Moreover, many of the
familiar moral and spiritual norms of social life seem to be
disappearing. Spiritual and moral evils, and I am not talking
only, or even predominantly, about sexual morality here, have
permeated society, and even found their insidious way into the
Church, to such an extent that they sometimes go
unrecognised.

In these circumstances radical measures are called for. These
measures, however, will not be the same as in the fourth and
fifth centuries because the conditions of modern life are different from those in post-Constantinian times. Instead of calling
people into the desert wildernesses far away from city pave-
ments, God seems to be asking people to find their deserts in
the heart of the towns and cities and is inviting them to 'pray
constantly' where they are,[18] and to resist evil through prayer.
Maybe God is calling so many people to such lives of prayer and
witness because that is one of the best ways of evangelising the
world. I believe that to be the case.

If enough people, scattered though they may be, pray in this
way then they will create a climate in which what was formerly
ignored, despised or scorned as a utopian dream begins to come
into society's consciousness. When that happens, it can effect
changes in people's attitudes towards many issues. History suggests that when such alterations of opinion do take place,
regarding slavery, for instance, or the role of black people and
women in society, then revisions of behaviour and social mores
follow, sometimes because of law reforms, sometimes before
changes to the law actually occur.

Another reason for the increase in this kind of call to prayer
as a way of life may lie in the fact that Western countries, such
as Britain, have become multi-faith communities. In general we know more about Judaic, Buddhist, Zen, Hindu, Sufi

and Muslim devotional practices today than our forebears did at the turn of this century. These and other religions are attracting new adherents. Consequently, Christians have had to look at their own tradition to recover confidence in their own beliefs and devotional practices.

As we approach the third millennium there are signs that Christians are now recovering their confidence in their own heritage. The past two decades have seen a great enthusiasm among Western Christians for retreats, conferences and workshops on prayer, the gifts of the Spirit, healing ministries and the links between prayer and personality. There has also been a decline in enthusiasm for the institutional ecclesial organised structures of denominational Churches. At the same time there has been a profound desire among many Christians to return to whole-hearted commitment to personal devotion for, and contact with, the Source of life and love.

It would be sad if this rise of interest in prayer and spirituality were to foster a growth in private devotion without a corresponding increase in social consciousness and prophetic action. There is unfortunately evidence that this is happening in some places. Spirituality is a growth industry and like all growth industries it can become tainted by materialism, individualism, narcissism, pietism and consumerism. Devotees can become so preoccupied with their own souls that they forget that the Church exists for the people outside it; they may ignore the call to mission, prophecy and pastoral care that is inherent in Christianity. So it may be that God is calling some of us to pray and live in alternative ways to help to bring the good news of Christ to those places where at present his Name is not known.

I am someone to whom this call to 'pray constantly' and to 'stand firm' has come. God has asked me to live this vocation in several different places and communities, and now I find myself living it alone but in companionship with other people who are called to 'pray constantly'.[19]

In the succeeding chapters of this book I have indicated some of the main evils of our own generation which need opposing in prayer, witness and action. In making my choice as to what to discuss, and how to approach the subject, I have chosen to discuss certain principles on which there seems to be general agreement among Christians rather than directly tackling the issues that stem from those principles. Christians have to work out for themselves how they put those principles into action. Although there are references to them in the text, I have deliberately chosen not to dwell on certain controversial issues which stem from those principles. For instance, I hold it to be obvious that for Christians all life comes from God and is therefore sacred. Nevertheless, Christians differ profoundly on the interpretation of this principle.

Although most people may agree that it is permissible to kill in self-defence, those who are convinced pacifists will not be able to kill under any circumstances. Some, perhaps many, Christians would allow abortion as a means of self-defence, at a personal and corporate level, but others cannot agree. Some would permit euthanasia; others abhor it. Some people would ban capital punishment; others feel able to condone it. Some can legitimate war, again on the same principle of self-defence: others hold it wrong to try to combat sin with another sin.

Similarly, I feel there is general acceptance among Christians that human sexuality is a precious gift to be used in ways that show love and respect for oneself and one's partner. In our present generation Christians are divided about whether or not it is morally permissible for Christians of the same gender to be sexually intimate with each other. Since I hold it to be more important to focus attention on areas of agreement rather than disagreement I have tried to use stories that point to the principles behind the illustrations rather than highlighting the issues.

My choice of evils to discuss has been a personal one; they are examples of the areas of modern life in Western society where I see most need today, and where I see God at work in many people's lives: doubtless there are others. My suggestions for active resistance to those evils are also personal. I am sure there are other equally good ways of doing the same task. I have simply gleaned some ideas from my own experience and from listening to other people who are walking along the path and offer them as a starting point for further debate.

❧

PART ONE

THE CALL TO PRAYER

CHAPTER 1

PRAYER AS A WAY OF LIFE

❧

Pray constantly (1 Thess. 5: 7)

More things are wrought by prayer
Than this world dreams of.
                    (Tennyson, *The Idylls of the King*)

RECENTLY THREE women were having a conversation about prayer. One of them was expounding on the difficulties of living a life of prayer. She was missing the structured protection of a monastic community.

'In a convent', she said, 'it's relatively easy to be aware of an on-going relationship with God. In a contemplative monastic community you keep on going back to chapel for Divine Office. We did that six times each day. You have access to a daily Eucharist. Your prayer times are protected from intrusion; out here in the world in an ordinary house, it's not nearly so easy, especially if you live alone.'

At that point one of the others might have said that one of the reasons people went to live together in community was to encourage each other; another was to ward off any intrusion that might interfere with their call to learn to live lives of constant prayer. They said nothing, however, because each of the three women was called to this same task without becoming a nun in community. Moreover, each was trying to do this in different circumstances. One was living in the country, another in a small and quiet town, the third in a large city. Two were 'retired' in the sense that they no longer had paid employment, so they could choose how active they wanted to be in local Church and local community life. The third woman was a hard-working curate in a large urban parish.

The oldest woman remarked, 'Out here in the world there's no one to help you to keep a good rhythm. There are all kinds of distractions. The doorbell rings in the middle of your prayer time. Do you answer it? You're out visiting sick people and suddenly realise it's past the time when you had planned to be at home interceding for the world. Does it matter that you're not keeping to what you had committed yourself to do? After all, you're not responsible to anyone but yourself for keeping to a rule about times of prayer and meditation. No one's going to come after you, as they would in a convent, if you don't turn up to a Eucharist in church.'

'It is difficult,' her retired colleague answered. 'Perhaps we need to find ways of encouraging each other to persevere. After all, not every Christian is called to pray constantly.'

'Oh, but we are,' retorted the youngest of the three. 'I have a struggle to get out of bed in the morning to say my prayers before the day starts in earnest and I don't usually have time to sit down during the day, but I feel called to be aware of God's presence with me all the time. All Christians are trying to pray all the time,' she added thoughtfully. 'There's nothing special about this call.'

Her companions agreed that there was nothing elitist about being called to a life of prayer, but they also thought that God might want some people to devote their lives to prayer, whereas God might call others to a life in which prayer was important, yet not continuous. These people might spend much time in practical and active expressions of their faith.

'It's not "either/or"', one of them said, 'it's a matter of finding the balance, according to what God wants.' At that point the conversation had to break off, and the three women went their separate ways.

I was one of those women. A few days later I went to see an eminent man of prayer, a noted spiritual director. I did not mention this conversation, but I did say that I was finding it difficult to maintain any conscious awareness of God's presence. I thought this was partly because I was having to live with the fact that many people were coming to my door with pressing needs for counsel, so I wasn't getting enough opportunity for the times of broody silence that usually help me to develop an inner attentiveness to God that can be carried over into the activities of each day.

He looked at me with kindly but stern concern in his eyes. 'Are you keeping to your times of prayer?' he asked.

'Yes,' I replied, 'just, but only God knows what's going on because I don't have any sense of Christ's closeness to me.'

'It doesn't matter,' he said. 'It's vital that you give that time to God and that you keep to a rhythm of prayer time. Too many people neglect times of prayer. They say that they are praying continuously whatever they are doing, but they're not, not with that kind of undivided attention you can get during prayer times. Those are essential if you are to learn to live a life of prayer.'

We finished on that note, but since those two conversations I have had time to untangle my thoughts on the relation between theological truth and experiential reality. It is a theological truth that 'we live, and move, and exist' in God (Acts 17: 28). It is also true that Christ lives in us (Gal. 2: 20) and that the Spirit dwells in us (1 Cor. 3: 16). Most of us, however, find it hard to hold on to a continuous awareness of that truth. Times of prayer, I believe, help us to make that theological truth an experiential reality.

When we become Christians, we are taught to pray, sometimes directly by God who draws us into prayer, sometimes indirectly by God through pastors who help us to find the tools we need to become aware of God's abiding presence with us. At first we usually find it easiest to learn during prescribed times of prayer when we go apart (Matt. 6: 6; 14: 23). In time we develop an ability to carry that 'secret place' with us wherever we go.

Jesus' command to 'go to your private room, shut yourself in, and so pray to your Father who is in that secret place' (Matt. 6: 6) and St Paul's instruction to 'pray constantly' (1 Thess. 5: 19), that is, to pray without ceasing, a phrase he uses elsewhere in his letters (Eph. 6: 18; Col. 4: 2; 2 Thess. 1: 11), and which is also to be found in the Pastoral epistles (1 Tim. 2: 8; 2 Tim. 1: 3), do not contradict each other. They are essential to each other. We need both the discipline of regular times of prayer and the acquired skill of focused attention that enables us to

remain centred on God, even in the midst of the bustle and
confusion of our ordinary lives.

Having made that statement, I must admit that such a task
is an exacting one for most of us who live in today's world.
True, there are a few groups of people who can secure good
conditions for their times of prayer, but for most of us it
is a struggle to make suitable provision for the time we need
to devote our full attention to God during our prayer times.
We shall also have to tussle with difficulties while we are
acquiring the skill to remain centred on God and while, at the
same time, we pay attention to the work in hand, or whatever
it is that is going on around us. So let us look at the ideal
conditions first, and then turn to those that most of us have to
contend with.

In affluent countries, communities and households it is relatively easy to learn to pray because if there is money to spare
there will be opportunities to buy books on spirituality and to
attend conferences, seminars and workshops on prayer. Those
who have reasonable incomes, or who are members of a
religious order where there is a reasonable communal income,
can probably secure adequate time and energy each day to
devote to prayer. People who are comparatively wealthy can
employ others to do the work that needs to be done while
they pray or study. Those who live in religious communities
can divide the labour of each day so that each individual can
have time to pray and also give time to work to release others
to pray. It is also helpful to be comparatively free from financial
anxiety because this is conducive to peace of mind. Thus one
can pay attention to God in prayer times; one is not afflicted
by hunger, cold or distracting anxieties; one knows where the
next meal is going to come from; one has the money to pay
the heating bills.

In our Western civilisation those kinds of conditions for prayer
now exist in very few households. Most of us who are employed
have to work hard for long hours each day. We are too tired to
get up early in the morning to pray, or to spend much time at
night in prayer. Those who are unemployed have to contend
with poverty, anxiety, tedium, and often with loss of morale
that may leave them disinclined to believe in God's sovereign

goodness. Those who have to look after small children are quite unable to 'go into our rooms and shut the door' during the hours when the children are awake, because to do so would put the children at risk. People who are old or afflicted by chronic illness do have the time to pray, but pain, weakness, mental infirmity take their toll, making prayer difficult.

These are realities in our time. So people who are called to prayer as a way of life must contend with difficulty and find their way through it. Their solutions to their problems often depend upon individual temperament and personal circumstances.

Some individuals who are called to pray continually realise how difficult that is going to be under the ordinary circumstances of life, and so they give up the social advantages of full employment. Instead they join a religious community where each day's activities are structured to provide them with opportunity to spend much time in worship and prayer. It is a fine and fulfilling vocation if you are called to it. In today's world, however, lifelong vocations to this way of life are not so common as they formerly were. Many people are called into religious communities to learn the disciplines that will help them to pray continually. After a time they may have to obey God by returning to the world to live out their lives of prayer in a different way.

Other people decide to go into full-time ministry. In this way they hope to find the right conditions to devote their lives to the worship and service of God. Some of these men and women, whose vocations are confirmed when they are accepted for ordination or stipendiary ministry, do discover ways of combining prayer and active service. Many who succeed do so because they live and work in teams where collective prayer is encouraged. Some establish collaborative ministries with lay people: mutual encouragement can be a great help in developing good practice regarding personal prayer and membership of prayer groups.

Most people, however, are not called by God to the religious life or to employment as ministers of religion. They have to do their best by going to church when they can and by spending what time they can each day in prayer. Many try to retreat from their ordinary work and lives from time to time to get themselves some space and time for more continuous prayer and reflection. Some of them may realise that they are thirsty for more silence and solitude than they are getting. They have to compromise. They are aware of a call to continuous prayer, but they don't know how to get the right conditions for it and so they put off responding to God's call until they retire.

Retirement undoubtedly brings the freedom to decide how to use time and if one has an adequate pension one is also relatively free from crippling mental anxiety. In the same way those who are left alone when their spouses die, or abandon them, may find it more possible to devote themselves to prayer than they did before. This has been recognised from very early Christian times in regard to widows. In the first Pastoral epistle to Timothy, for instance, we hear that 'a woman who is really widowed and left on her own has set her hope on God and perseveres night and day in petitions and prayer' (1 Tim. 5: 5). Christians of that time thought so highly of prayer that they were prepared to support such women, although they also laid down some stringent conditions for their enrolment:

> Enrolment as a widow is permissible only for a woman at least sixty years old who has had only one husband. She must be a woman known for her good works – whether she has brought up her children, been hospitable to strangers and washed the feet of God's holy people, helped people in hardship or been active in all kinds of good work. (1 Tim. 5: 9–10)

The freedom to withdraw from paid employment, or the independence that comes from finding oneself quite alone, yet still comparatively fit and healthy, may be significant; these factors may explain why so many Churches have more middle-aged and elderly members than young people in their congregations. Ministers of religion are inclined to see these people as 'freed to serve'; unhappily many vocations to continuous prayer may be lost because younger retired or widowed people are swept into a frenzy of good works. Initially, activity may help people to endure the sense of worthlessness and loneliness that often overtakes those who are made redundant at an early age, or have retired from satisfying work, or are devastated by bereavement. Ultimately, however, overactivity may be a distraction from their real calling.

Older retired, widowed or single people are often seen by pastors in Christian Churches as in need of help: they are seldom regarded as valued members of the Church who can make a positive contribution to the life and active mission of their local Church. So they may find themselves relegated to a backwater, cut off from effective communication and deprived of the sense of worth that comes from being an active participant in a lively Church congregation. Christians who are retired, ill or infirm are, I believe, numbered among those who are called to devote their lives to God in prayer. All Christian Churches need to value the potential that there is in such a group of people and to encourage it to be fulfilled.

These are some of the ways in which individuals who are called to live lives of prayer manage the difficulties that are inherent in such a call. Many people, however, cannot 'leave all' and join a religious community. Others do not feel called to ordained or stipendiary ministry. Some do not want to wait until they retire. Their call to prayer is too insistent for them to compromise to that extent. They have to find ways of surmounting the obvious difficulties that they may encounter.

Christians in leadership roles in all the denominational Churches need to pay serious attention to the difficulties that modern people have in securing adequate time and opportunities for prayer and study. It has to be said that all too often overworked and overstretched people still find themselves encouraged to pray in ways that are unsuitable for busy people in a world that is approaching the third millennium.

It is useless to urge people to pray if you don't take their circumstances into account. It is no use quoting the example of John Wesley, who said that he had to pray for three hours early each morning[1] to get through his busy day, to an exhausted worker who knows that Wesley was an exceptional man of great energy but that she or he, the worker, is a very average ordinary person who needs much sleep.

It might be uplifting to an audience of people who are eager to learn to pray to hear that Michael Ramsey, a former

Archbishop of Canterbury, found that during an hour's prayer time it took fifty-nine minutes' effort before he could get one minute of pure adoration and attention to God, as I once heard him say. However, many people in the audience might never have the luxury of an hour by themselves to focus their attention for fifty-nine minutes.

It might be suitable for a member of the clergy to say a regular Office, but to encourage employed workers to say Matins and Evensong on the bus or train on their way to and from work may impose considerable strain on the person who tries to do that. True, such practices may help someone to feel satisfied at fulfilling such an obligation, but the criterion for undertaking such a daily task is not personal satisfaction but personal growth in love of God. If reading an Office in that way helps anyone to grow in love for God and neighbour it is a productive enterprise that should be undertaken, or continued. Nevertheless, such devotions may hinder the growth of continuous awareness rather than fostering it. Perhaps there are more effective ways of reaching a continual awareness of God?

Anyone who questions the received wisdom of spiritual practices that may have been appropriate to people in former times, or may still be suitable for some people today, as I am doing, must, I believe, find the roots of their alternatives in scripture.[2] If they measure what they want to suggest against scripture they may find themselves in error. It may, however, be the case that the Holy Spirit will show them how to retain a principle while encouraging them to adapt it to changed circumstances.

By looking at a few examples of how the New Testament Church thought about prayer and action we might find an underlying principle that could help Christian disciples who are alive today to find ways of living that will allow prayer to feed into action: in turn action will feed into prayer. I have necessarily selected certain key passages because they have spoken so strongly to me in my own search for an authentic personal lifestyle.[3]

In the fourteenth chapter of the gospel of St Matthew, for instance, we see Jesus reacting to the news of John the Baptist's death by taking his disciples 'to a lonely place where they could be by themselves' (Matt. 14: 13). He is stopped on the way by large crowds and he turns aside to heal them their sick, and to feed them. At the end of the feeding of the five thousand, 'to say nothing of women and children' (Matt. 14: 21), Jesus 'went up into the hills by himself to pray' (Matt. 14: 23). He returns to rescue his disciples, to heal the sick and to confront the Pharisees who accuse his disciples of breaking with 'the tradition of the elders' (Matt. 14: 22–15: 20). Matthew's account of Jesus' movements suggests that Jesus gave up his desire to be alone with his disciples for the sake of needy people, and the fulfilment of his mission. He then tried to spare his disciples by sending them off in a boat ahead of him, so giving them some time to recover. He, however, was not deflected from his intention to pray: knowing his need, he went away to be with his Father before coming down again to the people who required his help (Matt. 14: 23).

We see the same kind of pattern of prayer and action fulfilled in a rather different way after Jesus' death and resurrection, when Peter and James are on their way up to the temple 'for the prayers at the ninth hour' (Acts 3: 1). They turn aside to heal a cripple from birth. They get arrested, imprisoned and put on trial and are then released. Immediately, they 'went to the community' (Acts 4: 21ff.). We who read this account many years later are treated to a vivid description of intense corporate prayer. The Christians who heard their story 'lifted up their voice to God with one heart' (Acts 4: 23). At the end of that time of prayer 'the house where they were assembled rocked. From this time they were all filled with the Holy Spirit and began to proclaim the word of God fearlessly' (Acts 4: 23–31).

Going a little further into the story of the Acts of the Apostles, we find an account of how the leaders of the Church found themselves getting overburdened by people's demands on their time and energy and by the great increase in the numbers of disciples who were attracted to the faith. They divided the work and kept prayer and the service of the word to themselves, appointing seven deacons to undertake the duty of 'handing out food' to the widows and the poor (Acts 6: 1ff.). Interestingly, this did not stop Stephen from 'working miracles and great signs among the people' (Acts 6: 8ff.). Moreover, he went on to serve the word by debating and preaching so eloquently that he was tried and executed (cf. Acts 7).

Another story from the New Testament seems to me to have relevance to modern Christian spirituality. It is the account in Luke's gospel of Jesus having dinner at Martha's house. In this story it is good to hear of Jesus' praise for Mary who, he said, 'has chosen the better part, and it is not to be taken from her' (Luke 10: 42). At the same time we need to recognise that he was not telling Martha off for her activity in preparing a meal. He admonished her because, as he said, 'you worry and fret about so many things' (Luke 10: 42). If Martha had been a little more organised she, too, might have been able 'to sit at Jesus' feet'. If she had not been jealous of Mary she might have learnt more through the happiness of knowing that her work had released Mary to listen to Jesus.

It sounds as if Jesus knew that Mary couldn't do two things at once. She needed time with him then. He praises her for her single-mindedness, yet, as every contemplative knows, no one can sit endlessly. After a time, Mary would have had to get up, eat, clean the house, wash clothes and do the ordinary, everyday things we all have to do to survive. It is not a matter of extolling 'listening' at the expense of those who make it possible for people to have the leisure to listen. Rather, it is a matter of encouraging ourselves and others to find or make the time to listen to Jesus at appropriate times and in suitable ways. It is a matter of learning not to fuss when we can't get that time because of urgent duties, such as preparing food for a tired and hungry itinerant preacher whom you have invited into your home for a meal.

These stories about Jesus and his disciples emphasise the difficulties of getting time to pray either alone or in corporate worship. They suggest that if the word of God is to be preached effectively there must be adequate time for listening to God. They encourage us, who read these accounts so many years later, to recognise that we need to use time wisely. We need time for personal prayer, for corporate prayer and mutual up-building in the Lord. We need time for study. None of these can be let go of completely. So in any alternative patterns of spirituality these elements should be present; not, however, in

the same way as was possible in more leisured times, nor necessarily as is still possible for members of religious orders and
sometimes for clergy and lay people who are devoted to monastic or cathedral-type worship.

So what might these rhythms of prayer that foster a continual
awareness of God, an awareness that is not necessarily fully
conscious, but is there in the background of one's whole life, be
like? What will help busy people who have the determination to
pray constantly, but who have relatively little time to spend in
formal prayer?

CHAPTER 2

PRAYER FOR BUSY PEOPLE

❦

Be persevering in your prayers, and be thankful as you stay awake to pray. (Col. 4: 2)

Our souls should be directed in God, not merely when we suddenly think of prayer, but even when we are concerned with something else. If we are looking after the poor, if we are busy in some other way, or if we are doing any type of good work, we should season our actions with the desire and the remembrance of God. (St John Chrysostom, Homily 6 on Prayer)[1]

BY THE TIME I was thirty-eight years old, I had four lively children under the age of six. My husband was recovering from an operation. My mother was living with us as she was slowly dying from cancer. I had a full-time job. Although I employed people to help me at home, I was stretched to the limit.

Until that year, I had done what many devout Anglicans of my generation did: I said morning and evening prayer; I usually attended a Eucharist two or three times a week. Quite often, I managed to get time for half an hour's prayer during the day. That prayer rhythm suited my husband, who was a priest, and it suited me.

That kind of Christian life came to an abrupt end when both my husband and my mother were in different hospitals ten miles apart. During the next two years I seldom went to church, never said any formal prayers and was tired out for most of the time. Yet it was during those difficult years that I began to learn new ways of praying. I realised that if I was to heed Christ's teaching about 'the need to pray continually and never lose heart' (Luke 18: 1), I would have to find ways of praying that were suitable for those with crowded lives.

30

What follows is a distillation of some of the things I learnt during those two years. Although later, after my mother's death, the pressures on me eased slightly, life remained more busy than I would have liked. Over the succeeding years I received a great deal of help from other equally busy Christians. I have added some of their insights to my own.

Going to church on Sundays is not an optional extra for Christians, something we tack on to our lives of personal devotion. It is one of the chief ways by which we witness to our faith and find inspiration, nourishment and strengthening grace for our work in the world outside church. It is also important to meet with other Christians so as to discover the richness of our diversities within the Body of Christ, visible and invisible. The tradition of each denominational Church, local custom and personal preference will usually decide how often we will attend the Eucharist and how frequently we will receive Holy Communion.

While many of us desire to, and can manage to, get to church every Sunday, churchgoing is not essential to a life of communion with God. If, for some good reason, Christians cannot get to church for corporate worship, then they are not cut off from God. Those who are obliged to work on Sundays, those who are imprisoned, or who find themselves isolated because of infirmity through age or chronic illness, or through having to care for small children or sick relatives, are not outside the Body of Christ. They are always able to be present at the Eucharist that is eternally celebrated in heaven. They remain part of their local congregation. Their worship is united with that of all other Christians. This does not excuse the clergy and people of their local Church from doing their utmost to visit and take word and sacrament to such people, but it does mean that no one should necessarily feel unable to live a life of continuous prayer if they do happen to find themselves physically separated from the main body of their local Church.

When we cannot get to church we can at least read the Bible prayerfully every day for about five minutes. Such reflective reading of the Bible enables the words of God to sink into the fibres of our being where they rest until the Holy Spirit prompts them to surface to full consciousness. Study, or using a devotional commentary, may be desirable, but is not essential.[2] If there is time for nothing else in each day, one should, I believe, fight for this five minutes of reflection.

We can also make use of short prayers at different points in the day to collect our thoughts and focus our attention on God. There is no need to carry around a Bible, psalter or Office Book, labour to find one's way through it, worry because one is inattentive to the written words on the page, or get upset because of inevitable interruptions. These prayers come spontaneously: they consist of remembered phrases from scripture, the Lord's Prayer and murmurs of adoration that arise from the heart.

To establish a good recurrent rhythm such prayers need to be said at regular times, at any rate initially. God does not need to hear our prayers at set intervals, for God is always aware of all that we are, and say, and think: rather, it is that we need to hear them so as to deepen our attention to the word of God. Perhaps no more than two minutes each time need be devoted to this activity, either in the morning and evening, or with the addition of noonday prayers and prayers said immediately before going to sleep. After all, it's not the amount of time one gives to God but one's yearning to be with God that matters.

This kind of verbal prayer is complementary to the reading of scripture. It strengthens one's memory of scripture and creates in oneself an attitude of listening. It helps some of us to realise that we are joining in a continual paean of praise with the angels and the saints, living and dead. It puts us in tune with the recitation of the Divine Office, a labour of love that in modern times is largely left to members of religious orders, clergy, employed ministers of the Church and people who have sufficient time and opportunity to join in the regular, formal, liturgical worship that is undertaken for the sake of the Church and the world.

Nevertheless, the time may come when an individual finds that he or she can dispense with all such forms of verbal prayer. It is often difficult to know when to give up such prayers. It is, therefore, good to talk it over with an experienced person of prayer before letting such a regular rhythm drop. When words do give way to silence, it is still important to find regular

occasions for quiet. Becoming quite still, even if it is for only
five minutes each time, two, three or four times a day might
replace said prayers and be very beneficial.

The use of scripture and short prayers are helpful practices
for those of us who are learning to pray continually, while at
the same time having to live busy lives. There are three other
activities that seem to me to be vital to the nourishment of
those who pray in these circumstances. These are the acquisition
of interior silence, the ability to be attentive and a willingness
to become a place where reconciliation can happen.

Finding Interior Silence

It is my belief that the whole purpose of trying to live a life of
prayer is to adore and wait upon God, to listen for that 'light
murmuring sound' of God's voice (1 Kgs. 19: 13), and to
discover what it means for our lives today. God is always faithful,
so we are never apart from God: becoming silent and attentive
simply helps us to discern what God is doing in us and in the
whole of creation.

While it is true that God can speak to anyone at any time,
and can overcome any obstacle, as happened when Peter had
his vision on a rooftop in Joppa and was persuaded by God to
associate with Gentiles, an idea that was previously abhorrent
to him (Acts 10: 9–29), it is also true that God does not deal
with most of us in that way. We have to learn to be quiet
enough inside ourselves to listen attentively for that 'light murmuring voice' despite what is going on outside. That is not
too easy to do in an industrialised Western society. There is so
much external noise and bustle going on. There are so many
terrible things happening in the world. Life is lived at such
speed. Changes are always taking place: they happen more
rapidly than they used to in our forebears' time. Noise from
outside penetrates and disturbs us.

It is not surprising, therefore, that many people think that if
only they could get away to a restful place they would automatically get quiet. This is not necessarily true. Going to stay in a
quiet place, such as a convent or retreat house, may be of help
initially, but, as so many people have found out from experience,

the wonderful external silence may simply set loose noisy thoughts and a whole series of turbulent feelings that come from inside oneself.

What, then, does help to overcome these real difficulties? There are two main ways of achieving inner silence. Both are simple and can be done anywhere, at any time, but they require the discipline of practice. The first is visual, the second auditory.

In the first method, one simply makes a mental picture of a place one has been to, where once one has felt utterly peaceful, and goes there again in imagination. I have several places like that to which I can now go whenever I want to. One is a stretch of coastline in East Sussex where I can sit on a cliff-top and look at the horizon, far out to sea. One is a quiet corner of a garden where my husband used to sit in his old age, with his cat on his knee and our dog asleep at his feet. Another is a dark corner in a church in Assisi. Having got there by mental recall and felt the enveloping still peace of that memory, I simply stop thinking about it and begin to enjoy the reality of the silence beyond the image.

Here is the hard part of this kind of exercise. It is not easy to let ourselves be taken beyond the image into the silence and stillness. We have to be content to wait in the images until God takes us beyond them. Our part in the venture is to yearn to be taken into that silence and stillness of which the psalmist speaks when he says, 'Be still and know that I am God!' (Ps. 46: 10). Perseverance will bring its reward. God will open the door and draw us into the heart of silence where we will find Love.

The second way of searching for inner silence is to use a repetitive phrase, sometimes called a 'mantra', which will take one below the surface of consciousness to a still place. Some people utter the name of 'Jesus' or 'God' or 'Love' repeatedly until all thoughts other than this word have vanished from their mind.[3] Others use a longer phrase such as, for instance, 'Jesus Christ, Son of the living God, have mercy on me a sinner', or 'By thy wounds five, I thee adore: O let me love thee more and more', or 'Maranatha, come Lord Jesus'. They persist with these rhythmic words until they need them no longer, because they have reached the place where all words fall away into silence. Some people will keep their surface consciousness quiet by knitting or gardening and achieve the same sense of peaceful stillness in that way.

Here, too, it is difficult to get beyond the words themselves, or the feeling of peace that they induce, to the reality beyond. If we stop at the words, the thoughts or the feelings we get from them, we may enjoy the experience and come back from it quite refreshed, but we may not have gone through the door held open for us by God.

These experiences of silence are akin to sleep or death. We have to allow ourselves to lose control as we hand ourselves over to God. In this kind of venture it is what God is doing for us that is important, not what we are doing for God. We need to come to that still, warm, dark place of 'unknowing' with the confidence and faith of a small child putting her or his hand into the hand of a loving parent.

Those of us who explore interior silence usually find we need to practise, initially by setting aside times when we can be alone and uninterrupted. If we are faithful to our times of silence, to the point when we know that we can suspend our thinking for short periods of time, we shall discover that we can find that place of quiet again even if we are quite busy. One can, for instance, garden, knit, sew, paint, clean the house, cook a meal or do some mundane repetitive tasks while dwelling in this kind of silence. In time, we shall find that we can go in and out of that quiet place at will.

It is not, however, advisable to try to get to this kind of silence under certain circumstances. No one, for instance, should try it while driving a car, handling complicated machinery, performing a surgical operation or thinking about complex issues. Total concentration is needed for those kinds of activity; any form of divided attention is inappropriate. It is perfectly possible, however, for someone to return to the silence at suitable intervals during these activities. One can stop the car in a lay-by and get a few minutes' total rest. One can use one's tea break for the same purpose. It may be possible to switch off momentarily during a board meeting to find a quiet moment of stillness. Such short interspersed times of silence are refreshing and they clear one's mind. They do not necessarily lead to a conscious awareness of God's presence or to the yearning that we call prayer. Nevertheless, God is with us.

Some of the benefits of this kind of restful silence only become evident after we have emerged from it into renewed activity. There are, for instance, times when we become aware that the problem that exercised us so much only a few minutes ago has been sorted out in the silence. I certainly found this to be true when I was a busy general medical practitioner in a large urban practice. During morning surgery I would see one patient out of the door and before fetching the next I would put my head down on my desk and disappear for a moment into silence. Sometimes when I returned I would see more clearly what might need to be done next time I saw that person. Even when that did not happen, I would always find my mind clear and ready to greet the next client.

Although I might utter an arrow prayer before and after going into such a silence I would not call these momentary silences times of prayer, except in the broadest sense that my intention is to turn towards God 'in whom I live and move and have my being' (Acts 17: 28). The link between silence and prayer comes through trying to be attentive in the silence to what might come into that void.

Attentiveness

It is easy to talk about attentiveness as if all one had to do was to concentrate on God in thought and prayer: but it is not. If we try to be attentive to God in our prayer times we are likely to find that we are beset by distractions. Many of us find that when we begin to pray we are host to a thousand and one images and thoughts that seemingly have nothing to do with God. We may get worried by these distracting thoughts and feelings and seek ways of dealing with them.

One of the most sensible traditional solutions to this problem of straying thoughts is to suggest that all distractions and digressions can be turned into prayer and used by God. Indeed, there are times when I feel sure that the Holy Spirit does remind us of people and issues that need our intercessions and concern. Another tactic is to allow the distractions to float away, as if one were lazily lying on the grass on a hot summer's day watching a kite high in the sky. The kite is there, but since one is not flying it oneself one has but a passing frisson of interest in its presence. There is a third, currently less popular, solution: we can try to focus our attention on God to such an extent that we become quite unaware of any other presence.

In my own experience none of these stratagems is altogether effective. What I have found most helpful is to look for what God is doing in the immediate moment. This involves seeing two images at once. One sees the distracting image or thought clearly: simultaneously, one sees what God is being and doing in that situation. The ability to do this depends upon the very ordinary knack, which most of us possess, of being able to do two things at once. For instance, many of us can drive a car while we listen to music on the car radio or cassette. We can knit and read a book at the same time. We can even cook the supper while keeping an eye on a toddler in a playpen. We can garden and think about other things. Christians also develop this skill when they recite the rosary and contemplate the mysteries of certain episodes in Jesus' life, or when they look at a picture and think about God.

It is but a short step from that kind of activity to being able to relate what we see to our own lives. Some people are very good at doing this and making connections between what they see and what it means to the way they live their lives. One of the best-known examples of this kind of contemplative reflection comes from a twentieth-century monk, Thomas Merton. He was standing on the corner of a shopping centre when:

I was suddenly overwhelmed with the realisation that I loved all these people, that they were mine and I theirs, that we could not be alien to one another even though we were total strangers. It was like waking from a dream of separateness, of spurious self-isolation in a special world, the world of renunciation and supposed holiness. The whole illusion of a separate holy existence is a dream. Not that I question the reality of my vocation, or of my monastic life; but the conception of 'separation from the world' that we have in the monastery too easily presents itself as

a complete illusion: the illusion that by making vows
we become a different species of being, pseudo-angels,
'spiritual men', men of interior life, what have you.[4]

That kind of insight, however, is not enough: we have to move
from that kind of 'seeing' to the contemplation of God in the
harsher reality of our daily lives.

This is, I think, what the fourteenth-century anchoress Julian
of Norwich was doing when she contemplated her visions of
Jesus crucified. She beheld the reality of sin and evil; she saw
the fact of Christ's suffering; then she understood the meaning
of what she saw, in a way that enabled her to see what Christ
was seeing, and saying, about himself and about the world in
which she was living.[5] It is also what the prisoner at Auschwitz
was doing when he looked at a youth who was executed by
hanging. In his book of personal memoirs about his time in
Auschwitz, Elie Wiesel describes this event:

> The SS hanged two Jewish men and a youth in front of
> the whole camp. The men died quickly, but the death
> throes of the youth lasted for half an hour. 'Where is God?
> Where is he?' someone asked behind me. As the youth
> still hung in torment in the noose after a long time, I
> heard the man call again, 'Where is God now?' And
> I heard a voice in myself answer: 'Where is he? He is
> here. He is hanging on the gallows.'[6]

There is nothing new or specifically Christian about this kind
of 'double seeing'. It is a form of contemplative gazing on
God. God makes these disclosures; we receive them. There are,
however, ways in which we can attune ourselves to look for
the meaning in what we are seeing and try to discern what
God is doing now.

One good way of asking God to reveal the meaning of events
is to watch, or listen to or read the news in an open and
prayerful way every day, preferably twice a day. Doing this can
be as much a part of intercession for the world as any period
of prayer in church or oratory. In watching the news on television, for instance, we must face the reality of what we are
seeing and not shrink from it. We can take that pain, or joy,

into ourselves and offer whatever is happening inside us as a prayer. Then we should, I believe, go one step further. We need to ask God to show us what Christ is doing in that situation, and also whether we are being called to work with him in a practical way.

Let me illustrate the way in which this might work at a practical level. During the early part of 1995, I was watching a television news item about the way in which calves are sometimes reared for veal production. They are housed indoors, confined in narrow crates, fed a special diet and then killed. Some people were protesting about these manufacturing processes: the police were struggling to ensure that lawful consignments of live animals could be loaded on to aeroplanes that would take them out of sight and mind to European countries that allow this method of veal production.[7] Now the animal lover in me abhors such treatment of young animals. The practical woman in me recognises that farmers need to make their living by selling calves for veal production.

As a Christian I watched that news item, asking myself what God was doing at that moment. Probably others were also asking the same question, and the answers they received may have been different from mine. These are the thoughts that went through my own head as I watched. God cares for all creation, making no distinction between the calves, farmers, protesters, viewers. God suffers with creation. Men and women are made in God's image and so they carry that stamp in themselves and have a special responsibility regarding creation.

As I prayed, I found myself yearning for a more humane method of farming to become the 'norm' in all parts of the world as well as in Britain where such methods of rearing young animals are forbidden by law. Then I asked myself, as I always do, whether I myself was called in conscience by God to get directly involved in the work of promoting better ways of treating animals. The answer was 'yes' in the sense of prayer and intercession, 'yes' in regard to not eating veal. I need to make some protest and that is a reasonable action. I said 'no' to active involvement in the protests at the sea ports. But it might have been 'yes' to everything, and has indeed been so over other issues. It's not a matter of giving priority to one issue over another, one form of activity over another. All that matters is that one puzzles over the meaning of news items, prays, asks the Spirit to reveal what God is doing and wanting to be done in the situation, and then tries to respond in prayer and action.

There is, admittedly, the danger of becoming overwhelmed by one's own attempts to use everything that happens each day as an invitation to prayer. It is easy to get flooded out with other people's problems and sufferings, especially if real people are also turning up on one's doorstep rather than coming into the house through the television screen or radio. Each individual can only do so much without having a physical or nervous breakdown. It is precisely because there is so much need for prayerful involvement in today's world that I believe that God is calling many more people today to live lives of prayer at the heart of the world. Each person does a small amount, but when each individual contribution is put together the sum of their devotion is great.

The ability to attend to whatever is happening in our own environment is a skill that can be acquired by learning to be observant. In itself, it is not necessarily a gift from God. I believe, however, that we do need the gift of the Holy Spirit to be able to make connections between what we observe and what God is doing. If we persist in prayer, we shall one day come to a place where we see what the Holy Spirit is doing in each situation. For if we go to the heart of God in still, silent attentiveness, we shall find that we are not alone. The whole world is there with us. We shall see everything and everyone in God, not, perhaps, exactly as God sees them, because our human vision is imperfect this side of death, but see it all the same with eyes of love. The closer we are to the heart of God, the clearer we shall see, the more we shall be able to listen to creation groaning with desire for 'the same glorious freedom as the children of God' (Rom. 8: 18–23), and overhear the murmuring of the Spirit 'in accordance with the mind of God' (Rom. 8: 27).

It is not enough to confine our activity to that of prayer. Prayer should spill over into our domestic and working lives. Christians are called to be co-workers with Christ for the coming in of the Kingdom of God. We may fail to fulfil our potential, we may shun silence, we may refuse to listen to God, but, as Christians, we are baptised into Christ. We go down with him into the waters of baptism: we suffer and die with him; we are raised with him; we are given the gifts of the Holy Spirit and sent out into the world to proclaim the good news of salvation to others.

It is my belief that we all have a unique task to fulfil, a task that is given to each of us, and to no one else, on the day that we are conceived, yet paradoxically a task that may be shared through collaboration with other people. One way in which some people are called to work for the sake of God's Kingdom is to 'become a place for reconciliation'.

Becoming a Place for Reconciliation

If, as I suspect, God is calling many people to live lives of prayer in the world, then I also think that one of God's purposes is to invite more people to become places where Christ can do his reconciling work.

It is a theological truth that baptism incorporates us into the Body of Christ. St Paul puts it neatly: 'I have been crucified with Christ and yet I am alive; yet it is no longer I, but Christ living in me' (Gal. 2: 20). Christ's indwelling presence with us means that, through the Holy Spirit's work in us, we can become aware, as Gerard Manley Hopkins was, that Christ 'Easters in us'[8] and that 'his power to save those who come to God through him is absolute, since he lives for ever to intercede for them' (Heb. 7: 25). We also know that Christ has reconciled all things to God 'by making peace through his death on the cross' (Col. 1: 20; cf. Eph. 2: 11–20). We know that since Christ's ascension into glory he has continued his work through his disciples. As St Paul says: 'God has entrusted us with the message of reconciliation' (2 Cor. 5: 19).

Christ is always winning the victory, and we are always being called to be his ambassadors (2 Cor. 5: 20), but there are times when human beings, including Christians, seem to be doing their best to hinder that reconciling work. Interdenominational disunity, squabbles within denominational Churches, the dehumanising ways in which people can treat others, frenetic activity, preoccupation with self-gratification, consumerism, materialism, individualism, the pollution and exploitation of the environment and rampant territorialism all present obstacles to Christ's reconciling work in the world. We who are Christians are sometimes as guilty as non-Christians of these sins against God. So there is, I believe, a great need for repentance and conversion of manners among Christians.

The Spirit is calling many among our own generation to that kind of a change of heart. When we truly turn to God we can become places of reconciliation for the sake of the Kingdom, places where we witness in our own bodies to an alternative way of living. To become places where Christ can do his work of reconciliation means accepting conflict as part of life. This is because Christ does his work on the cross. There he brings his divinity and his humanity together and allows the cosmic struggle between good and evil to play itself out in full force. It is on the cross that he wins the victory.

We who are Christians, who are his Body, his temple, the place where he continues his work in our own generation, will sometimes know ourselves to be a place of conflict, a place where the battle between cosmic powers takes place, a place where we become part of the struggle 'against the principalities and the ruling forces who are masters of the darkness in this world, the spirits of evil in the heavens' (Eph. 6: 13). However one regards that evil in the heavens, whether it is seen as the collective evil of humankind or a demonic evil, or both, it is a reality of life.[9]

It is a reality that one can only face with faith, the kind of faith of which St Paul speaks in his letter to Christians at Ephesus when he tells them to 'take up all God's armour' (Eph. 6: 13) and urges them to 'stand their ground' (Eph. 6: 14). I used to find Paul's use of military language quite difficult to take on board because I do not believe that we should ever use force against force, but I now recognise that spiritual combat is not the same as making war against creation because its only legitimate weapons are those used by Christ and reiterated here by St Paul.

The succeeding chapters of this book attempt to look in a

realistic way at some current evils in Western societies, and at the practical ways in which they can be resisted by Christians who pray.

PART TWO

❧

STANDING YOUR GROUND

CHAPTER 3

SEEKING THE TREASURE

०‍‌‍‌‍‌‍‌‍

Set your hearts on his kingdom first, and on God's saving justice, and all these other things will be given you as well. (Matt. 6: 33)

Vereker's secret, my dear man – the general intention of his books: the string of pearls were strung on, the buried treasure, the figure in the carpet. (Henry James)[1]

ONE MORNING when I went to my local newsagent to buy the paper, I found it unusually crowded. People were queuing up at the counter and the line snaked itself double, filling the space in this quite large shop. It took me a few seconds to realise that it was the first day when tickets for the National Lottery in Britain could be sold. The people in the shop were waiting to register and pay for their tickets.

The manager knew me.

'Do you want to buy one, Sister?'

'Thanks, but no,' I said, adding hastily, 'not that I've got anything against it, but I haven't any money on me.'

The moment I said it, I knew I was not telling the whole truth. I had said those words for several reasons. First, I didn't want to sound priggish in front of a friend. Second, I didn't want to declare my own views then. Third, I wondered what people would think if they saw a habited nun buying lottery tickets. Fourth, I've never liked to gamble, although my Church permits it and encourages its members to buy raffle-tickets at church fêtes. Fifth, I knew that for a small stake one *might* win a huge sum of money and I thought that if that happened to me I'd be corrupted by it. Lastly, and it's notable that this reason came sixth on the list, I remembered the words in St Matthew's gospel, 'for wherever your treasure is, there will your heart be too' (Matt. 6: 21).

Many Christians would have had no trouble at all over buying a lottery ticket. They'd have seen it as a bit of harmless fun, a way of helping charities. They might daydream about what they would do if they won a large sum of money. Most people who had bought tickets that day would enjoy themselves on the Saturday night when the results would be declared on nationwide television. They would feel a flutter of excitement, but scarcely any disappointment if they didn't win, a mild frisson of envy perhaps? After all, only one person out of fourteen million people would have the problem of what to do with a huge win.

I went out of that shop chastened, but also thoughtful. Did I need to re-examine my views on gambling? What did the phrase from the Bible that disturbed me actually mean? Could I win a great deal of money and not be corrupted by it? Could I keep my treasure in heaven while owning a large sum of money? Other people presumably did, so what was my anxiety about?

I didn't know. The next week I decided to see what would happen if I bought a lottery ticket. The prize money was higher because no one won the 'jackpot' the first week. The queues continued. I joined them. That felt quite comforting. Filling in the form was easy. Payment for one 'game' was modest. There was virtually no guilt. The pipe dreams were quite pleasant. I enjoyed the Saturday night entertainment and was mildly relieved when my numbers did not come up. Later, I felt sorry for the man or woman who won seventeen million pounds that week. Then I watched the subsequent uproar over the unwanted publicity with dismay.

This small episode led to more questions. It also made me think more deeply about gambling than I had done before. True, I had come to no harm through my small 'flutter'. Some charitable cause had benefited from a share in my stake: but what if someone, who could ill afford it, had gambled their rent money on the lottery? What if a winner's happiness was destroyed because so many of his or her friends became jealous, envious, accusatory? What if winners felt they were too rich to go on working? What if losers were tormented by greed, envy, critical thoughts to the point where friendships were destroyed? What if people stopped giving money to small charities because they thought that all they needed to do was to gamble on the National Lottery?

These were important questions. Trying to answer them led me to re-examine my own opinions about the kind of society I belong to. If society puts so much emphasis on monetary treasure, do its moral values suffer? If, as the proprietors of the National Lottery suggest, people invest more whenever they know the prize money is higher than usual, should society allow that kind of incentive to continue? To do so may be pandering to our collective greed for personal wealth irrespective of what is happening to other people. There is a good argument for enabling more people to win, even if each successful gambler wins less than a sum like seventeen million pounds! If we use money as a symbol of value, by what criteria do employers in society select who is to earn huge sums of money and who is to earn a pittance? Should those of us who have more than sufficient share what we have with others who are poor? Is it right that some countries should be getting richer at the expense of others which are getting poorer? Should a desire for high wages, the trappings of wealth and status in society dominate our attitudes towards money? Should the demands of the consumer dictate the supply, or are there other considerations that should be taken into account? Are the issues only about money, or does acquisitiveness affect our behaviour in other spheres of life?

The questions are endless. Many Christians and other people struggle with them valiantly. Most of us can work out individual solutions about the stewardship of our own possessions. Many of us share some of our income with those who are less advantaged than ourselves. Fewer of us are concerned about the morality of our society in regard to wage structures. Some do get involved in discussions and action about the government of the day's policies on the care of the unemployed, homeless, sick and destitute people of our land. Relatively few of this last group of people seem to worry about our national policies

towards other countries of the world. Mercifully some do; their
interventions prick our individual and corporate consciences.

Some people are relatively indifferent to money. They can
do without wealth, but they want status and honour in society.
They will sell their integrity to gain public approval, an honour
or a knighthood in the annual awards list. They will ignore the
needs of the poor to curry the favour of the rich. They may
even betray their ideals in order to win the temporary approval
of people they formerly considered to be in error. Such people
are making as much obeisance to worldly gain as those who
consider money to be their god. Some of them may even flaunt
poverty as a cover for avarice of a different kind. These people
are as greedy as those who seek wealth. None of us, even those
who are content with a modest income, are immune from these
kinds of attitude. Those of us, like myself, who know just how
easy it is to fall into sin in these ways, and who do not like
that trait in our own characters, have to find ways of dealing
with the acquisitive attitudes that can coexist with detachment
from a love of money.

I am not, however, immediately concerned with the practical
solutions that can be found to answer some of these questions.
Instead, having made some assessment of where the problems
about what we treasure are, I want to be attentive to what God
is saying about money, possessions and avarice through scripture.
It seems important to know how to pray about these issues.
Christ laid such emphasis on these issues about money and
stewardship of talents and possessions. He obviously knew how
easy it is to become someone 'who stores up treasure for himself
instead of becoming rich in the sight of God' (Luke 12: 21).
If we want to 'sell everything we have' to buy the 'treasure
hidden in a field' (Matt. 13: 45–6), if we want to set our hearts
on the Kingdom first (Matt. 6: 33), then we will want to know
where and how God wants each of us to change.

The Bible says quite clearly that nothing on earth is permanent. Treasures on earth can be destroyed by moth and wood-
worm. Material goods can be stolen by thieves (Mat. 6: 19–20).
Scripture teaches us that if we try to accumulate wealth, we
may die before we have time to enjoy it (Luke 12: 16–21). We
learn that we must be prepared to leave material goods to

follow Jesus (Mark 1: 16–20; Matt. 19: 16–21). We read that
the Kingdom of God is like 'treasure hidden in a field', or 'a
pearl of great value', which someone wants so much that 'he
sells everything he owns and buys it' (Luke 13: 44–6). We hear
that you cannot be the slave both of God and of money (Matt.
6: 24), but we also learn that wealth and gifts of skills are not
evil if we use them in a right way (Matt. 25: 14–30).

Jesus' stories, example and teachings urge us to have compassion on the poor and to share what we have with them
(Luke 12: 33–4; Luke 10: 25–37). The writing and example
of the apostles Paul and James teach us about the goodness of
earning our own living, being generous to others and treating
everyone with respect, independently of their wealth and status
in society (1 Cor. 9: 1–18; 16: 1–4; Phil. 4: 10–20; Jas. 1:
9–11). James is particularly clear in his condemnation of those
who allow class distinctions to influence their behaviour.

The Bible is also strongly against setting ourselves up on high
(Ps. 75: 5), and in favour of humility, as shown in the story of
the Pharisee and the publican (Luke 18: 9–14), and in the one
about the two brothers who wanted to sit at Jesus' right hand
(Mark 10: 35–40). If we seek God's Kingdom, if our desire is
to put our treasure in heaven, then our hearts will be there
also, and our behaviour will match God's desire.

Christians, listening to these words and praying about them,
have come to all kinds of decisions. Some Christians have
definitely decided that their treasure *is* in heaven, so they
have acted on that principle in a literal way. They have 'left all'
to follow Jesus. They have endured material poverty, lived in
simplicity, learnt to detach themselves from preoccupation with
either wealth or absence of riches. Men and women who have
abandoned riches often live heroic lives of sacrificial love and
humble service of God. They can be a shining example to
those of us who are encumbered with goods and anxieties
about our possessions, honour and status, although we do not
necessarily feel called to follow their example. The figure of
John the Baptist, for instance, stands out as someone who had
'left all', and who also knew that he must stand aside and 'grow
less' so that Jesus could 'grow greater' (John 3: 30).

The number of people who live in this way are relatively

few. Some of them worry those of us who still have our feet firmly on the ground because they do not feed themselves properly, they do not heat their houses, they may even live by the kind of faith that expects to be kept by those of us who are still earning money. Those who join religious communities and give up all personal possessions may forget how much things cost, because they no longer have the personal responsibility of buying goods. Instead, that is done for them by one or two senior officials in the community. Moreover, the community itself may be wealthy. Such a community may be able to afford to buy expensive goods for the use of its members, or send them to conferences and retreats that individuals living alone or in families could never afford. Paradoxically, too, the more material possessions one gives up, the more likely one is to acquire a liking for less obvious possessions such as authority, honour and high status. Certain kinds of material poverty can be dangerous to our souls. They can even blot out our ability to store our hearts and our treasures in heaven (cf. Matt. 6: 19–21).

So, on the whole, I do not find that those people who have 'left all' can be of great help to me in knowing what to do about the use of my own money. They certainly do not help me to know 'how to live modestly', and 'how to live luxuriously too' (Phil. 4: 12).

They do not help me to know what I could do to stand against the materialism and consumerism that now appear to underlie social life in my own country. They do not help me to combat the feeling of helplessness that comes over me when I consider the complexity of the issues with which we have to grapple in modern society. They do not always help me to be happy whether I am 'pulled down' (Luke 1: 52) or 'raised high' (Luke 1: 52). They do not help me to know how to live my life if I want to witness to alternative Kingdom values as a disciple of Jesus.[2]

The people who have most helped me to untangle issues about money, possessions and stewardship of talents and gifts have been those who have been able to face the complexities of life in a materialistic consumer society, yet who are always pointing us to the need for justice for those who are impoverished by the current systems which prevail in our world. People like Dorothy Day,[3] who got her hands dirty by living with the poor, suffering with the poor and engaging in political and social work on behalf of the poor, have had a considerable effect on the way I live. The writings of people like Charles Elliott[4] have helped me to understand the difficulties of knowing how to respond to the inequalities and injustices of our society. In his book *Praying the Kingdom*, for instance, he draws attention to the immense difficulty in knowing whom to approach for redress of injustice. He says:

> The most powerful single mechanism for removing well-being from one group and bestowing it upon another seems to be beyond the control of *any single group*. Producers do not control prices. Consumers don't. Despite much populist comment, in most cases multi-national corporations don't. Each may have some influence, and that influence may be unequal. There is, however, no one single authority; no equivalent to a planning committee which makes an unambiguous decision; no identifiable 'them' to whom one can talk or against whom one can rail.[5]

Charles Elliott and, in a different way, the author Richard Foster[6] help me to root personal action in prayer for the coming to earth of the Kingdom of heaven.[7]

Charles Elliott puts this prayer into context:

> Prayer for the Kingdom transcends the partialities of any political position we can define for ourselves. In that sense, it is dealing with ultimates rather than proximates, with eternal dimensions rather than temporal situations. That does not mean it ignores the real to concentrate on the unreal, or that it is so heavenly minded it is no earthly good. It is simply to recognise whose Kingdom it is, and that we honour the King.[8]

To seek for treasure in heaven, to pray 'Thy kingdom come, thy will be done, on earth as in heaven', does not necessarily mean being otherworldly. It means that we are asking for a different kind of society on earth than the one we have now.

As Christians who pray every day 'Thy kingdom come, thy will be done', we have to think through what we are saying when we pray those words. When we pray them we mean, I hope, that we want a society on earth that mirrors what goes on in God's Kingdom. We are asking for a just and compassionate society, one in which the good things of the world are shared, one in which the rich people and nations of the world share their wealth with those who are least able to fend for themselves, one in which everyone puts their neighbour's welfare before their own, one in which we know how to rejoice with those who are rejoicing and how to weep with those who weep, one in which people treat each other with courtesy, concern and compassion.

Christians can and should pray for all who are affected by the monetary policies of world governments. We can pray for our local communities, for people who are still employed and for those who are being made redundant. We can pray for those who are put out of work by modern technological advances. It is right to pray for our local communities and for individuals in monetary difficulties, or who have a lot of debts. It is helpful to pray for people who are lured into overspending by advertisements. People who are very rich, prominent in society or famous – all those who are 'riding high' – also need our prayers. We can pray systematically, or more spontaneously, whenever these issues and people come to mind.

Money has its uses. Ownership can be compatible with seeking treasure in heaven. Those of us who are still working can be thankful for our earnings. Pensions are a boon; they mean that we can take care of ourselves. We should be equally thankful when wage-earners' taxes can help us when we are out of work, for whatever reason. Having money is a responsibility that may be burdensome, but it brings us close to other people, and helps us to be mindful of the needs of others. Those of us who are Christians are able to share whatever we feel to be a fair proportion of our known income with those who are less advantaged. We can use what we have left wisely. That may indeed mean saving up for a special holiday or conference.

As consumers we do have some power, even if it is not as

great as we like to think it is. We are free to buy goods that
are manufactured in other countries by firms which pay their
employees just wages. We need not buy food or goods that
depend on cruelty to animals for their production. We may
prefer to buy recycled goods. We can, if we wish to, boycott
certain foods and firms that exploit vulnerable people in other
countries. Some of us choose to spend more money in small
shops and firms than we would do were we to buy the same
goods in a supermarket. In these ways we can help to reduce
local unemployment, preserve corner shops, encourage small
firms. We can create demand by asking for food that is healthy.

We also have power as protesters. We do not need to judge,
criticise or use force of any kind against other people, but we
can write letters to newspapers and firms. We can, perhaps,
join a peaceful demonstration, or stand outside a supermarket
to ask shoppers to donate goods for starving peoples in other
countries. We can also ask our members of parliament questions
about consumer and monetary issues. Sometimes we may even
feel so strongly about a particular concern that we decide to
lobby parliament.

There is, however, more to the prayer 'Thy kingdom come,
thy will be done on earth as it is in heaven' than intercession for
those in financial difficulties, or those who have to implement
difficult monetary policies. So far, I have written mainly about
treasure as if it were definable in terms of money and material
possessions. There are, however, other kinds of treasure that
corrupt us and prevent us from being able to do what Jesus
told his disciples to do, namely, 'Set your hearts on his kingdom
first, and on God's saving justice, and all these other things will
be given you as well' (Matt. 6: 33).

Those of us who think that we are seeking treasure in heaven,
that we are detached from any desires for material wealth, are
very likely to find that we are attached to 'spiritual' treasures
of our own making. We may hold on to our good name,
defending it against even valid criticisms. We may hold on to
our 'special' job in our local Church, or our particular role in
the PCC, thus denying anyone else a chance to use their skills.
We may even pursue status in our Church when we should be
content with a more lowly place. We find all sorts of subtle

excuses for doing the things we are doing. We may convince ourselves that there is no one else who can do a particular job and so we justify keeping it. We may label the task as 'undesirable' and feel virtuous for retaining it. We may rightly feel that there is no one else who could do the task as well as we are doing it. In offering these excuses to ourselves we are, perhaps, denying ourselves the opportunity to enjoy the spiritual treasures of generosity and humility and to store them in heaven. It is surprising, and sometimes a little disappointing, how often someone suitable does step forward as soon as they know for certain that one is definitely retiring!

It is my belief that those of us who are called to resist evil, to pray and to witness to our beliefs should ask God for insight into our own attitudes towards money, status and honour whenever we attempt to do anything about the injustices we see happening to other people. Through prayer we will be challenged by the Holy Spirit in areas we least expect. Once we have begun to sort ourselves out we have some hope of being less judgemental about other people's attitudes towards material wealth and possessions.

Through prayer God teaches us not to judge other people, or society, but to resist what we see to be wrong for ourselves by our attitudes and actions. In consultation with like-minded people we can find the support and encouragement that we need to help us to persevere with our good intentions.

Prayer changes our attitudes. Prayer prompts us to personal action. Our prayer, united to that of other people, can help us to create a climate in which change becomes possible, then feasible, then achievable. These good effects of prayer begin with individuals and move into the communities and societies in which the individuals live.

The choice of what to do, or not to do, is for each person to make. All that I am suggesting is that if we ask God to show us what our treasure is now we will be shown. If we ask where we are storing that treasure we will be given an answer, providing we are honest enough to hear it. If we ask for the grace to set our hearts on God's Kingdom and saving justice first, our prayers will be answered. If we then ask what we can do to bring in the Kingdom, we will be led in the right direction.

Much of what I have been saying is a matter of Christian common sense and sounds rather prosaic, but underlying our attitudes towards treasure there is one treasure that cannot be dispensed with in our lives, love. There is a love story by Isaac Bashevis Singer which shows us how love can help us to locate our treasure.[9] It is a children's story about two old leaves, Ole and Trufa, who are the last to cling to their branch as winter comes. Ole falls to the ground first and Trufa is left on the tree. She mourns, longs to fall to the ground, pleads with God to let her die. Cruelly, nothing seems to happen, but one day she awakes to find herself on the ground:

> She knew now that she wasn't just a leaf that depended on every whim of the wind, but that she was part of the universe. She no longer was small or weak or transient, but a part of eternity. Through some mysterious force, Trufa understood the miracle of her molecules, atoms, protons, and electrons – the enormous energy she represented and the divine plan of which she was a part. Next to her lay Ole and they greeted each other with a love they hadn't been aware of before. This wasn't a love that depended on chance or caprice, but a love as mighty and eternal as the universe itself. That which they had feared all the days and nights between April and November turned out to be not death but redemption. A breeze came and lifted Ole and Trufa in the air, and they soared with the bliss known only by those who have freed themselves and have joined with eternity.[10]

That kind of love, the kind that all of us instinctively know to be real, is the kind of relationship that can exist between God and ourselves and it transforms all the small things we do into acts of love within God's Kingdom. If indeed we put the Kingdom of God first in our lives and store our treasures in heaven, then we are brought to the 'bliss known only by those who have freed themselves and have joined with eternity'. That freedom and love are made visible on earth by the way we pray, live and witness for the sake of the Kingdom of God.

It is the Holy Spirit who prompts us to prayer, helps us to turn towards the greater good and enables us to witness to our beliefs. Speaking for myself only, I have decided not to play the National Lottery again. I realise I might well have come down on the other side of the argument. I make no judgement on those who feel it is all right for them to play, but it is not so for me. It is a small witness to make but to play again would not be consistent with my personal belief that my heart's desire is to seek treasure in heaven.

CHAPTER 4

THE JOY OF BELONGING

৶৻৶

Now Christ's Body is yourselves, each of you
with a part to play in the whole (1 Cor. 12: 27)

We don't live alone. We are members of one
body. We are responsible for each other. And I
tell you that the time will come when, if men
will not learn that lesson, then they will be taught
it in fire and blood and anguish. (J. B. Priestley)[1]

ANTHONY WAS a technocrat, a computer 'whiz-kid'. When
he left university with a good degree he and his family
thought he would get a job quite easily. He didn't.

He was short of money so he lived with his parents. Some
money came in from unemployment benefit. The local library
provided him with daily newspapers. Seventy applications each
week went off to various firms. Six interviews followed. In
each case his qualifications were commended but he didn't
secure the post.

After six months Anthony was despondent. He was being
urged to look at less skilled employment. The employment
office offered him the opportunity to retrain; he knew he
would soon have to accept. During the six months he had
worked as a volunteer in a local residential home for mentally
disabled adolescents. He liked the work.

At this stage Anthony's morale was low. He couldn't understand why he was unable to secure employment. The family
doctor whom he visited had no such problem. Anthony wore
thick glasses, walked with a slight stoop, was hesitant in speech
and diffident in manner. The doctor thought that her patient
was unlikely to interview well. Other candidates would have

the advantage over him, even if his paper record was good. In a highly competitive society he would slide to the bottom.

The doctor decided to risk a frank discussion, knowing that Anthony's morale might dip even further once he knew how he appeared to other people. She need not have worried. As soon as she broached the subject of his appearance and manner he relaxed with relief: they discussed ways of getting round the difficulties. The doctor recommended him to the local psychologist and suggested he might like to join an assertiveness training group that met at the nearby leisure centre.

The psychologist discovered that Anthony had never felt that he belonged in his family. He was not his mother's son. He was her grandson: he had been adopted by his grandparents after their daughter had given birth to him at the age of fourteen. He had grown up thinking that his mother was his older sister. He was a teenager when he was told the truth. It was a terrible shock.

The psychologist and Anthony embarked on a long course of therapy. His morale improved. He began to apply for jobs again. At the fourth interview he landed a job.

He stuck it for three years, but as time went on he realised that he wasn't going to get promoted. All around him people were busy 'climbing the ladder of success'. As individuals some of them were delightful: one even became a good friend. But as competitors they were ruthless and highly motivated. By this time most of Anthony's contemporaries were married and had mortgages to pay. They needed promotion. Some were overextended financially and were desperate for higher wages. Anthony was not married. He was still living at home. His morale began to sag again.

He went back to the doctor. 'Have you thought of a change of work?' he was asked.

'Yes, lots of times. I don't feel I belong anywhere. Home is no place for me to be now. I need to be out on my own. I've tried to find a partner, but I haven't done so yet. I'm still so shy, you see. My firm is so huge, it feels impersonal: I don't feel I'm valued there. As for society, it just devalues my contribution. If you measure success by money and status, then I'm always going to be classed as a failure.'

Anthony's story does have a good ending. He found the courage to explore alternatives to paid employment in a competitive market. He began slowly. He volunteered to work at the residential home for mentally disabled young people on Saturdays. When he had been there for some weeks he met someone who spoke to him about the L'Arche communities,[2] where assistants and residents with learning difficulties live together and belong to each other. Anthony decided to investigate, liked what he saw and then threw his job up. He joined a community at some distance from where his parents lived. He is still there five years later. He gets paid a small allowance, a pittance by commercial standards. The community of which he is a member has given him so much that he has become more confident. He no longer measures himself against the values that currently prevail in Western society. Moreover, he is happy. He feels he belongs.

The 'Anthony' in this account is not one person. He is a compound of several people, whose privacy I have taken pains to protect. I have, however, written about real people and real events in their lives. The sequence of events is not untypical of what can happen to such people. Such stories do not always end so happily. Another possible ending would have been that Anthony became unemployed again, a 'failure', a 'drop-out', a 'scrounger' in the eyes of many of his contemporaries and perhaps even in his own. It is highly unlikely that he would have outmanoeuvred his competitive rivals, but I suppose if he were desperate he might have done that too.

This tale, complex though it is, as real-life stories usually are, illustrates the miserable 'downside' of life in a competitive society. Those whose childhoods are marred by severe trauma, bewilderment or rejection often find it difficult to feel confident as adults. Men and women who look different from other people, or who present as less self-assured at interview, may have problems finding employment in a competitive environment. People who are vulnerable, or who are weak links in a chain, often go to the wall. We who live in an industrialised society are so used to its competitiveness that we scarcely recognise what it does to us, whether we are materially successful or find ourselves labelled as failures. It takes rare courage to challenge the system.

Anthony's story illustrates all these points and yet the issues raised are even more complex than I have described because there are, as always, benefits as well as disadvantages in being a member of a Western industrialised society. It is these very advantages that lead to the ills of individualism, by which I mean the practice of the doctrine that the interests of an individual should take precedence over the interests of other people, groups or society as a whole.[3]

Western industrialised societies offer high rewards for those who are able to fight their corner. It is possible to achieve a high standard of living through talent, flair, hard work and merit. The right to work, to earn a reasonable income, to achieve success in one's career, to feel good about being able to provide for oneself and one's family, to be treated as an individual with ambitions and needs, exists and should be honoured. Yet in order to achieve wealth and status in society those who aspire to such success may have to climb to affluence over the backs of other people. To some extent this is likely to happen to every person who lives an ordinary life in a Western society because the economy of such a society depends on competition.

Competitiveness itself is not wrong: it only becomes so if one rates one's own interests so highly that one is willing to ignore other important relationships, both in one's own family and in the community or society to which one belongs. If one overrides all other considerations and puts one's own interests first then one may be guilty of individualism.

This evil creeps up on people. The people in Anthony's firm, for instance, may have been reluctant at first to see Anthony and others go to the wall, but after a while they may have been so thankful to retain their own positions that they could not spare much thought for those made redundant. Out of this group of survivors a few may go further. They begin to pull rank, denigrate their peers and use questionable methods to secure their next promotion. They may even begin to despise weaker people and relish defeating their competitors. They have begun to forget that they have a duty towards their neighbours. They have become individualists.

In time such people find allies. Then groups of individualists perpetuate class distinctions, professional elitism, exorbitant wages for themselves at the expense of the people whom they are supposed to be serving. After yet more time the ill effects of individualism become institutionalised so that certain groups in society find themselves oppressed by others. In Western society, for instance, the rights and dignities of certain classes of people – women, blacks, homosexuals, disadvantaged men, women and children and the mentally disabled – have been ignored by their oppressors – men, whites, heterosexuals, advantaged and mentally well-equipped people. The oppressed have been expected to be silent, compliant, grateful for any sign of compassion or understanding of their feelings.

In these circumstances it is not wrong for the oppressed people and those who have their interests at heart to stand up and ask for their human rights. Rather, it is essential for the oppressed to seek justice so that their oppressors can be liberated from their blindness, complacency and inhumane behaviour.

It would be natural for such oppresed people to think that Christians would be among those from whom they could find strong support. After all, the Church's doctrine is clearly favourable to the rights and dignities of human beings. Since they are part of creation they are wholly dependent on God for their existence (Gen. 1: 1—2: 4a). They are given stewardship of creation (Gen. 1: 28–9). Moreover, they can enjoy the covenant relationship that God established with all creation (Gen. 9: 8–17). When Jesus came on earth to bring the new covenant to God's people he also brought about their reconciliation in his own body and by his death (Col. 1: 21–3). He taught people to love, serve and cherish each other (John 13), and to be concerned about each other's welfare and needs (Matt. 25: 31–46). He asked them to be considerate towards their neighbours to the point of being good Samaritans to their enemies (Luke 10: 29–37). Jesus encouraged his followers to accept any talent or skill that can be used to bring in the Kingdom and that might be of service to the whole community (Matt. 25: 14–30; Rom. 12).

The Church of the New Testament is clearly opposed to oppressive individualism. Christians belong to God in whom they find their unity and community with each other. The Church is the Body of Christ (John 15). St Paul uses the image of a body with different parts all having a share in its effectual working (1 Cor. 12). He points out, 'if one part is hurt, all the parts share its pain. And if one part is honoured, all parts share its joy' (1 Cor. 12: 26). The early Church acted for the collective good: 'the whole group of believers was united, heart and soul; no one claimed any private possessions, as everything they owned was held in common' (Acts 4: 32).

Succeeding generations have tried to preserve the strong sense of community that existed among Christ's disciples in his own time and in the immediate years following his death. They are still trying to do so, but unfortunately, in practice, individualism can exist within the Christian community. It is a fact that from the time of the foundation of the Church, and throughout its history, the Church has been a collection of sinful people who are as corruptible as their neighbours who are not Christians.

Individuals within the Church may seek power within a local congregation by insisting that their points of view have precedence over the desires of the majority of their community. They may behave in such a difficult way that clergy and decision-making bodies give in to their unreasonable demands so as 'to keep the peace'.

Clergy may act in ways that oppress laity: they can use a freehold as a power base; they may show no concern about their neglect of the evident talents of the laity. Groups of clergy can act together to ensure that those with whom they disagree are kept firmly subordinated. A strong minority may try to use collective voting power to keep at bay any changes in ecclesial structure with which they disagree. The fact that they can defend their actions by appeal to belief and conscience does not justify some of the unfair tactics they use to achieve their goal.

Church congregations too may act in ways that clearly show that they are putting their own interests above all other considerations. A whole group within a congregation or community can act as if it were an individual. It can exclude, reject, isolate or oppress people who threaten it. In subtle ways groups can exclude or reject people who don't fit in with their norms to the point where the individuals they oppress feel obliged to leave. Sadly, an entire local Church congregation can in certain circumstances become a closed community, an elitist group of self-satisfied people who do care for one another but who are quite ignorant of the needs of those outside their doors. They may exhibit some features of community among themselves but they have forgotten that the Church exists to serve those outside it. They have forgotten John Donne's word: 'No man is an *Island*, entire of itself... any man's death diminishes *me*, because I am involved in *Mankind*; And therefore never send to know for whom the *bell tolls; it tolls for thee*.'[4]

An entire denomination of the Church may act as a closed community without concern for its fellow Christians. It excludes people except on its own terms. Denominational interests keep Christians divided from each other. The scandal of our disunity gravely weakens our ability to witness to our love for each other in Christ.

Christian community can be as infected with individualism as an impersonal secular institution or section of society. There are occasions when belonging to a tight-knit community can result in the kind of unthinking and unswerving loyalty that leads to disaster. As St Teresa of Avila puts it, 'Cursed be all loyalty that goes so far as to impinge on one's loyalty to God.'[5]

Many of us who are alive today will have been witness to the results of tribalism in sectarianism, gang warfare, terrorist activities and genocide. So the solution to the problems of a society infected by individualism does not necessarily lie in specific forms of communal life such as closed communities, nor in communes, nor in communist states, because all these community-building exercises may be open to corruption by the very evils they are seeking to withstand.

It is, however, my belief that Christians have much to offer the world in the fight against individualism in all its various forms because they find that when they belong to Christ they belong to everyone else in the world. That kind of belonging can and does offer an antidote to individualism in all its ugly aspects.

The Christian Answer to Individualism

The Christian Church began when Christians committed themselves to Christ and found themselves drawn into a living Body, a Body in which we are 'all one in Christ Jesus' (Gal. 3: 28), a Body in which we are to express our love for each other through our mutual love for the Lord (Col. 3: 5–17).

As Christians, our sense of belonging begins with our commitment to Christ. Christ, our head, draws us to himself, for:

> . . . in him were created all things
> in heaven and on earth:
> everything visible and everything invisible,
> thrones, ruling forces,
>   sovereignties, powers –
> all things were created through him and for him.
> He exists before all things
> and in him all things hold together,
> and he is the Head of the Body,
> that is, the Church. (Col. 1: 15–18)

Once we give our lives to Christ we are brought into contact with a person in whom the whole world is to be found. This means that we will find ourselves relating to everyone else in the world. We belong to each other. Most of us, however, do not recognise this fact as soon as we become Christians. Our sense of unity with everyone in the world and, indeed, with the cosmos has to develop through personal experience of a truly open community. It grows on us through prayer, particularly the prayer of intercession, and through the experience of joining a local congregation, or a group within that congregation. Since in Christianity the material and the spiritual belong together, it is natural that this experience of true belonging will usually be rooted in a local congregation.

When we first join a local Church, we are unlikely to feel that we belong straight away. We are still on the edge. We are dependent on other people making us feel welcome, at ease, at

home. Often we have to wait to be invited to make a contribution to the life of the community. If the Church is a welcoming one then we shall begin to find our place in it. We shall
begin to help where we can. We may join a prayer or study
group.

Even if we do not do that, we may gradually find that we
are becoming part of the life of the whole congregation. It is
then that we begin to feel that we belong. Once that has
happened and, I think, not before, we become willing to relin-
quish our own desires if they seem to clash with the good of
the whole community. We begin to want to be loyal to the
expressed desire of the whole rather than to cling to our own
preferences. We begin to put other people's wishes before our
own without necessarily forsaking our own opinions. We begin
to love the group to which we now belong, and that love
endures.

Moreover, this sense of belonging which may begin with
one other person, one small group, one small congregation of
Christians is more contagious, once it starts to happen, than
the evil that it expels. People who have been harmed by society
are healed. They begin to value themselves. They find themselves able to survive competition, rejection and diminishments
that are imposed upon them in an individualistic society. They
begin to resist the evils of competitiveness and individualism
by the manner in which they live their lives. In time they will
change other people's attitudes that feed into individualism.

So many people in societies like our own, which are fragmented, materialistic, individualistic and uncertain about where
they are heading, are seeking to belong to another person, a
family, a group, a Church. Many have very little previous
experience of true community. Some have none at all. Unless
they can find it in a local Christian congregation they may
never have any experience of what it means to belong, never
feel that sense of warmth and loyalty that comes from being
cherished, loved and needed. So it is imperative that Christians
everywhere take on the task of becoming so like Christ, the
head of the Body, the Church, that we can mediate his love to
those who have never experienced it.

Practical Ways of Gaining a Sense of Belonging

Learning to belong to any group that is larger than oneself is no easy task. It is made easier if the group is open, friendly, confident in its own identity and, therefore, able to look for growth without expecting total conformity. It happens more rapidly where the group to which one aspires knows the meaning of love and takes its direction from the Source of all love and life. Belonging to any family or group does not mean that we are exempt from disagreement, argument, even anger with each other. Far from it: it means that if we know we are loved, and belong, we can survive all these ills. It means that we can show mutual respect for individual differences in temperament and need. We find that we can stay together, even if we disagree profoundly. It means that we will want to try to find ways around our disagreements and difficulties. Ultimately, it means that we have a chance of making Christ's reconciling work visible to the world.

Acceptance has to be mutual. It is impossible to belong unilaterally. However much we long to become part of a group, however loyal we are, however loving we are, we will not belong unless the person or group to which we want to belong accepts us. However much the group wants to accept the outsider into its midst, that cannot be achieved without the willing consent of the person or people whom the group wants to include.

None of us can accomplish this task by our own strength. St Paul has given us a glimpse of the enormity of the task, the hope by which it will be fulfilled and the fruits of this endeavour of love:

As the chosen of God, then, the holy people whom he loves, you are to be clothed in heartfelt compassion, in generosity and humility, gentleness and patience. Bear with one another; forgive each other if one of you has a complaint against another. The Lord has forgiven you; now you must do the same. Over all these clothes, put on love, the perfect bond. And may the peace of Christ reign in your hearts because it is for this that you were called together in one body. Always be thankful. (Col. 3: 12–15)

This kind of belonging together in one body is, I believe, one of the most important challenges and tasks facing the Christian community today. In order to achieve the kind of community of which St Paul speaks in his letter to the Colossians, each small Christian group or community must take its strength and lead from Christ, the head of the Body, the Church (Col. 1: 18).

When any individual finds a congregation, group or community that looks welcoming and joins it, there is usually a testing period as he or she waits for acceptance. If, through the gentle exercise of trust and perseverance, all goes well, the individual and the group will one day discover that they belong to each other.

One of the best ways of finding each other is through silent prayer in a group. The Fellowship of Contemplative Prayer[6] and the Julian groups, started by Hilary Wakeman,[7] have done a great deal to promote corporate silent prayer. The silence may last for only a half an hour or, at most, an hour, but the effects of such shared silence last much longer; they foster a loyalty that helps people to return again and again. Silent retreats achieve the same feeling over a period of days, but unless one is with a group of friends or people from a parish, they cannot easily foster a permanent sense of belonging to a group.

If, even once, a person who has a shared experience of prayer feels that he or she belongs to the others in that group, the feeling of belonging can be carried into times of individual silent prayer.

Dietrich Bonhoeffer once said: 'Let him who cannot be alone beware of community. Let him who is not in community beware of being alone.'[8] I remember a nun rephrasing this saying by telling me that 'no one who cannot get on in community should be a solitary, and that no one who cannot be alone should join a community.' It is certainly true that there is a strong link between solitude and togetherness, between a solitary person at prayer and a gathered community at prayer. Finding the balance may be difficult, yet it has to be done if any group is to grow. There has to be space for people to be alone, to feel secure on their own, yet if we are not to get isolated or lonely, there has to be the knowledge that we are, in fact, never alone. We are a gathered community within the Body of Christ and in time we shall know ourselves to be one with all who are alive in God on earth and all who are alive in God in heaven.

The realisation of our oneness in Christ should ensure that any small group within a larger one does not become isolated from the whole body. For too long Church leaders have been afraid that small groups can become elitist and so divide the whole. Such fears may prevent individuals and small groups from finding out about the joy of belonging to each other, lest 'they divide the whole body'.[9] It is a fear that can only be cast out by trust and love, but there can be no success without that leap of faith that prompts us to seek, and to go on seeking, the joy of belonging.

The joy of belonging cannot, however, be bought at the cost of conscience. The development of mutual loyalty and real love take time, and perseverance. When any group of disparate people try to live together, make corporate decisions, struggle to find a common direction, there are difficulties. These are inevitable. If loyalty to a Christian group is to be encouraged then all concerned must respect the rights of individual conscience, but all must also submit that conscience, in all things save sin, to the process of discernment as to what is God's mind in any particular matter. This is where most of the difficulties about belonging occur. This is where irrational argument or prejudice can masquerade as individual, or even collective, conscience. This is where a majority decision may do injustice to a minority group. This is where we may hesitate to go on belonging to a group whose views seem to be incompatible with our own.

In a partnership, whether it be that of a married couple, a couple who live together under the same roof, a community, or a Church-related group, there has to be considerable determination to stay together, despite difficulties, if the partnership is to be successful and enduring. St Paul goes so far as to encourage us to exult in our hardships:

understanding that hardship develops perseverance, and perseverance develops a tested character, something that gives us hope, and a hope which will not let us down, because the love of God has been poured into our hearts by the Holy Spirit which has been given to us. (Rom. 5: 4–5)

I have been describing the ideal. Many people who belong to local Churches, small groups or communities might well take me to task because their congregations or groups are not ones that engender a sense of belonging, security and loyalty. The fact that it is difficult to attain an ideal should not deter any of us from seeking it, for some groups do come near to reaching it because they invoke God's help and rely on grace in their dealings with each other. It is worth the effort involved to try to belong and go on belonging, even if the organisation to which we want to belong falls short of perfection.

Nevertheless there has to be, I think, a time limit on any struggle to belong to a particular group. The time limit may vary from person to person, group to group, but in my experience it takes up to two years to feel that one belongs anywhere, and anything up to five years to discover that one does not belong. If there are no signs that one belongs within two years, one should seriously consider leaving. If one does decide to persist, and there are no signs of mutual acceptance and trust within five years, one should probably leave. Not to do so is likely to be damaging to oneself and destructive to the whole group. This has nothing to do with forgiveness. Forgiveness has to be limitless. Rather, it has to do with individual and group growth. 'Shaking the dust off' our feet is also scriptural (Matt. 10: 11–16).

However, it is to be hoped that many people who come to the doors of a Christian Church community will find a warm welcome waiting for them and will discover the joy of belonging. Tribalism of any kind has no place in a Christian community, so people who rejoice in their belonging to any local group must always be looking outward to God's world and seeking to find themselves neighbours to the whole world in God.

'Anthony', whose story heads this chapter, found his worth as a human being in a community of people whose hearts grew warm towards him. L'Arche communities are sometimes like that.[10] Like their crucified Lord their arms are always open. Some L'Arche communities are shining examples of that kind of love. There are others: many house Churches, Franciscan tertiary groups[11] and Focalare groups[12] are places of welcome and belonging. Within all the Christian denominational Churches some local Church congregations and house groups show their love for God by the manner in which they love one another and those to whom they reach out. They are the hope for the future. They are the good yeast that may leaven the whole as the dough rises and the living Bread is shared with those outside the Church.

CHAPTER 5

FINDING OUR HUMANITY

❧

God created man in the image of himself, in the image of God he created him, male and female he created them. (Gen. 1: 27)

When God made man the innermost heart of the Godhead was put into man. (Eckhardt)[1]

ANNIE WADDLED up the long ward towards the locked doors and the doctor who had just come through them. Her hair was grey and matted. She wore a torn and faded nightdress. Her feet were bare. Behind her lay a trail of urine. She was shouting obscenities at her companions as they slumped in high-backed chairs, some with restrainer trays locked in place across their laps so that they could not get up. The ward smelt of faeces partly overlaid by disinfectant. Annie passed the doctor, shouted offensively and made for the doorhandle. She rattled it, pulled at it, pushed it, rattled it again, then began to bang on the door with a remorseless and persistent hammering. A ward orderly appeared, glanced at Annie and went away. A uniformed nurse came out of the bathroom, went up to the hysterical woman and gently tried to divert her from the battered door.

'Come on, Annie, it's time for your bath. Afterwards there'll be a cup of tea and a biscuit. Come on, love.'

'I'm not your love. Go away; I want to get out. I want to go home. Now. Home. Mummy, take me home!' Her wail rose to a screech: 'Mummy, mummy, mummy!'

The nurse took her in her arms, momentarily hugged her, and then firmly turned Annie towards the bathroom and marched her back down the ward.

It was the doctor's first day on duty in these locked wards. She looked at the Hogarthian scene before her and wanted to turn on her heels and walk out of that place for ever. Instead, she went over to a vacant armchair and sat down. She didn't know what to do. All she could remember was the time over twenty years before, when she had been a medical student. She had visited a psychogeriatric ward as part of her training. On that day she had been asked to care for a patient called Rosa. Rosa had spent the morning whining in a high-pitched voice for her mother at ten-second intervals. Like Annie, Rosa had wet herself. As the two of them made their way to the bathroom they had been met by a nurse.

'You're a naughty girl today, Rosa, playing up the young doctor like that.' Rosa had stopped, swung herself round to face the medical student and said in a clear voice: 'She doesn't like me and I don't like her; so there!'

It had been true then. Was it still true, I wondered, as I sat in my high-backed chair and thought about Annie.

By the time I met Annie I was forty-six years old. I had come to work in a psychiatric hospital after many years' experience as a family doctor. I had nearly completed my studies to become a deaconess of the Church of England. Thinking about this encounter with Annie, I realised how much I had changed. I was still afraid of senility and dementia, but I was no longer judgemental about the nurse's attitude towards Annie as I had been about Rosa's nurse. Twenty years before I had been indignant that the nurse should have spoken to an eighty-year-old woman as if she were a little girl. Now I recognised that Annie's nurse was speaking to someone who was real, Annie, the child who wanted her mother. In that child I could see the image of Annie as she had been when she had potential to carry the best of her child self into her adult self. I could see the unfragmented person she had once been. I could see the image of God in her. I could speak to that image. I could glimpse her humanity.

I was not yet sure that I had seen the most human way of responding to someone like Annie. After all she was not a child: she was a fully grown adult and needed to be treated by others with the respect and courtesy that any adult with the full use of her intellect has a right to expect. But I had begun to find a better way of relating to people who were suffering from an illness of which I was afraid. So I got up and began to try to find the persons behind the obscuring fog-like illnesses that were afflicting nearly all the patients in that particular ward. I began to try to find the person who, despite their illness, indeed, through their illness, was becoming the person Christ was forming them to be, if not here then in another mode of existence.

It is now more than twenty years since that encounter with Annie. I have retired as a doctor. Instead, I am chaplain to a small local hospital where we care for many elderly patients: some of them have Alzheimer's disease, a proper name for some kinds of dementia, and often a kindly euphemism for other kinds of dementia. I am no longer afraid of dementia for I am of the age when I know it may happen to me one day. It will be upsetting to the people who have to care for me, but for me it may be a kindly way of meeting the inevitable diminishments of old age. I can often find the person behind the broken minds of the people I meet. But when I can't do that I can still find out about the person who once lived, talked, loved, worked, reared children, was honoured in society. I can still relate to that person who is now apparently absent. And when that is impossible, I can still find the image of God in the fragmented person before me: I can still look to see what God is doing and will do for that person as they become fully human.

These changes in my attitudes towards people who have serious illnesses or disabilities which affect their personality are, I believe, due to God. God has led me, taught me, shown me the face of Love in ways that have helped me to find Christ's image in many of the people whom I now meet. It has been a gradual process, the fruit of much prayer, much listening, much observation of the ways in which people like Mother Teresa and Jean Vanier[2] treat the people for whom they care.

This account of my changing viewpoints over a span of forty years might be encouraging to others. They reflect the fact that our attitudes can and do change. The Holy Spirit does lead us into all truth; although I cannot say that I have now discovered truth in an end-time sense, I do believe that I am on the way. Learning to treat everyone as if they were what God means them to be, and is helping them to become, is, I believe, the only way that human beings can find a truly human way of behaving towards each other. In today's society such a task is fraught with difficulty.

The Difficulties of Finding Our True Humanity

In the Western world we live in communities and societies where civilised behaviour is under threat in many different ways. Men, women and children have become accustomed to antisocial behaviour. We all walk with fear of meeting someone who is not willing to, or able to, reflect the kind of humanity we want to see. The drunk wayfarer who once walked into my house taught me how vulnerable older women are when they are defenceless. It was very hard to find true humanity, that is, the image of God, in that man. The street lout who was threatening another with a knife suggested Cain rather than a child of God. The torturer can hardly be described as someone who visibly reflects the image of God. It is not at all easy to see God's image in the man who rapes children, the priest who abuses their trust. People who diminish their own humanity, and thus mar the image of God, abound everywhere. As William Law says:

> The difference then of a good and bad Man does not lie in this, that the one wills that which is good, and the other does not, but solely in this, that the one concurs with the living inspiring Spirit of God within him, and the other resists it, and is and can be *only chargeable* with Evil, because he resists it. Their behaviour can destroy other people's faith in the goodness of humanity and the sovereignty of God.[3]

People who mar the image of God in themselves often fail to see the image of God in others. Sometimes, however, they do, and then they may behave unpleasantly because they deliberately want to hurt God through destroying God's image in other people. We who are but human ourselves cannot judge such people. That is God's prerogative but, if and when they break the law, we can and do punish them according to the law. Our retribution may sometimes seem harsh, but it is a measure of our outrage at such behaviour, and must be understood as such. Yet excessive punishments can be a denial of our own capacity for evil: we prefer to punish other people for doing things of which we are capable in certain circumstances.

Perverse behaviour, such as I have just described, makes it harder for Christians to go on believing that all human beings are made in the image of God. Such negative thinking must be resisted, however, for if we come to accept that all people are inherently and invariably evil we shall gradually come to accept man's inhumanity to man as normal. When we are no longer outraged by antisocial or immoral behaviour, our own humanity is diminished. When we no longer protest when we see animals or other people being treated badly, when we watch the poor go to the wall, when we see the pitiable results of war between citizens of the same country, without undue concern, we are on the road to indifference towards other people's pain. We are abrogating our own humanity. We are colluding with evil. Whenever we fail to think of those whom we have oppressed as fully human, we ignore the image of God in them. In doing that we mar the image of God in ourselves. We denigrate our own humanity. So, for our own sake, it is imperative that we resist any behaviour that comes from our failure to see the image of God in ourselves and in others, however evil, unworthy or useless they may appear to be.

We cannot do that unless we are aware of how institutionalised these attitudes have become in Western society. People who are unemployed, people who are homeless, people who are disabled, people who are single parents, people who are black, gay or female, people who are old and poor are so often discriminated against in our society. It is as if society has decided that it needs to throw some of its citizens to the bottom of the heap. It selects those who are weakest to knock down, and makes sure that they never get up again. Those of us who are left standing are, not unnaturally, afraid of being knocked off our feet if we defend those in the pit, and so we do nothing. Yet there is a lot we can do.

Finding God's Image in Other People

Christians are people of hope. They cannot hold that any person, any group, any community, any society is irredeemable. After all, they have the example of St Paul who, when he was Saul, persecuted the followers of Christ, approved the killing of Stephen, and was still 'breathing threats to slaughter the Lord's disciples' when he started out on the road to Damascus (Acts 9: 1–2). He intended to take into custody 'any followers of the Way, men or women, which he might find' (Acts 9: 2). Instead he met the Lord.

What is remarkable about the whole story of his conversion is the way in which Ananias, despite his knowledge of Saul as an enemy of the Lord, despite his doubts that he argues out with the Lord, nevertheless heeds what God says to him through a vision. When the Lord indicates that Saul is a chosen instrument, 'to bring my name before gentiles and kings and before the people of Israel' (Acts 9: 15), Ananias does what he is told to do. He lays hands on Saul, heals him in the name of the Lord and either baptises him or witnesses his baptism. Ananias' action shows us that we must trust in God beyond what can be expected of human trust. If we listen and obey, God's desires will be fulfilled.

When the scales fell from Saul's eyes he could see again and his first action was to ask for baptism. Through baptism he found his freedom, his true humanity, his purpose in God's Kingdom. He became Paul, apostle to the gentiles.

In his writings Paul gives us the clue as to how we can become fully human and find other people's true humanity. His teaching, scattered about so many letters, notably in that to the Christians at Rome, can be summed up in some words that he wrote to the Christians at Corinth. Writing about our nature in the old Adam and our nature in the new Adam, Christ, he says:

> If there is a natural body, there is a spiritual body too. So the first man, Adam, as scripture says, became a living soul, and the last Adam has become a life-giving spirit. But first came the natural body, not the spiritual one; that came only afterwards. The first man, being made of earth,

is earthly by nature; the second man is from heaven. The earthly man is the pattern for earthly people, the heavenly one for heavenly ones. And as we have borne the likeness of the earthly man, so we shall bear the likeness of the heavenly one. (1 Cor. 15: 45–9)

Paul was speaking about what happens to us after death when 'this perishable nature of ours must put on imperishability, this mortal nature must put on immortality' (1 Cor. 15: 53), but since we know that our heaven begins on earth, that we are even now living in eternity, they apply to us who are still alive as well.[4] It is in bearing the likeness of the heavenly one that we shall find our true humanity. It is in seeing the likeness of the heavenly one in others that we shall find their true humanity.

How then can we, who are Christian, find ways of seeing that likeness of the heavenly one, the image of God, in ourselves and in others so that we can relate to it? Principally, I believe, through the prayer of intercession when we hold up to God our concerns about ourselves, others and all God's creation. We ask that God should do what is best for the people and/or the concerns that we are bringing to God, and we ask for our minds and hearts to be conformed to God's will.

Intercession brings us into touch with factual reality, with our feelings and with God. Every day we encounter people who need our prayers. In one sense intercession is an activity that can go on all the time, as we go shopping, watch the news on television, cook the dinner, go to work on a bus, saw logs for the fire. Our joy at good news, relief at finding someone we love is not going to die from cancer, our pleasure when a meeting goes well are, for instance, all occasions for thanksgiving. Our indignation, our angers at injustice, our sympathy for the victims of natural disasters, our empathy with the abused, divorced, bereaved people of the world prompt us to prayer. That kind of prayer should and does go on in millions of Christian homes all over the world.

All Christians are called to intercession. This is something we do in our personal prayers as well as in our corporate worship at church services. While it is true that God knows all our needs before we ask, and that Christ's 'power to save those who come to God through him is absolute since he lives for ever to intercede for them' (Heb. 7: 25), it is also true that every Christian is Christ's dwelling place, the space on earth where he abides and does his work. One can, therefore, say with confidence that God wants all of us to share in Christ's work of intercession.

If we put our heart into this kind of prayer we are likely to find intercession hard work. It is physically taxing and can be trying on the emotions. We may be tempted to suggest that specialists in prayer should be interceding instead of us. Alternatively, we may decide that our duty is done if we read a list every day. Sometimes we try to devolve all responsibility on to Christ. We simply lay the names before God in a book placed on the altar without giving that act the true support that it deserves, namely our intense prayer. Such prayer is a responsibility, not to be lightly undertaken. That is why some notable communities of healing prayer, such as the Iona Community,[5] ask all who send the Community names for intercession to remain in contact with those whose names they have put forward. The Community asks for regular progress reports.

Within that general ministry of intercession to which all are called, some people, very simple ordinary Christians among them, are drawn by God into involvement in a more intensive way. We may hear, for instance, of a relative, friend or neighbour who is in urgent need of prayer. We may have some experience of a contentious issue which appears in the newspaper headlines. We may be drawn by the Holy Spirit into intensive prayer for someone whom we only know through our contact with them via a news item on television or radio. This kind of focused prayer demands a more personal involvement, sometimes of a challenging kind.

Imagine that you are invited to pray for someone who has had a legal abortion. On receiving the request, you will be confronted by your own attitudes towards abortion. It may be that you abhor abortion under all circumstances. It may be that you can justify it under certain circumstances. It may be that you are neutral because you cannot believe that a foetus is a human being. It may be that you know the person and have a sneaking sympathy for her. It may be that you have had an abortion yourself. Your attitude will affect the way you respond. You may not be able to see the image of God in the woman who has terminated her pregnancy. Alternatively, you may be able to see it, but not see your own dislike of what she has done. You may be able to hold your distaste for what she has done together with your compassion for her as a person made in the image of God. Whatever happens in those first seconds after you receive a request for prayer will influence your response. In turn that will make it harder or easier for you to overhear what the Spirit is asking of you.

You may not be able to pray for such a person. That is a pity, but it may be the wisest response if you cannot find the image of God in a woman who asks for abortion, or in yourself. If, however, you do agree to pray, then what happens is that you take that person into Christ's presence and leave her there confidently before the throne of mercy and grace.

Is that all that happens? No, I don't think so, not always. Intercession that is undertaken with love does not leave the one who pleads unmoved or unchanged. An effect of this kind of prayer is that we are immediately confronted with our own evil, confronted with the realisation that we are capable of abortion, theft, violent protest, even of murder. We cannot find the image of God in other people who are sinners unless we can first find it in ourselves, even though we know our own capacity for sin. One effect of intercession is to make us more aware of our own fragility, more aware of God's mercy and, therefore, more tender, more compassionate, more forgiving towards ourselves and towards those for whom we pray.

Second, to give ourselves to intercession is to commend the person or issue we are praying about to the angels and saints of God so that their prayers can be added to ours. Then they and we surrender our charge into the care of the Holy Spirit who is always at prayer taking our concerns to Christ, our only mediator and high priestly intercessor. This 'letting go' that is a necessary part of such surrender helps us to become more humble about our own role in intercession. We who pray with hands held open towards God do so in God's strength, not ours. We become more relaxed as we learn to rely on God rather than on ourselves. We become more trusting towards God, whatever the outcome of our prayer.

Third, intercessors give themselves to being places where Christ may do his reconciling work on behalf of the world. If we are attentive we will hear what he is doing, we will 'put on the mind of Christ' (cf. Rom. 13: 14; Gal. 3: 27), we will overhear what God wants of us, and we will find ourselves able to respond to that call.

Having outlined some of the likely effects of intercession upon the one who intercedes, let me return for a moment to that request to pray for someone who had a legal abortion. It would not surprise me at all if, having prayed, you heard God inviting you to get involved, either directly with the person for whom you are praying, or indirectly with other women who are vulnerable in society and might need help. Or you might hear the Spirit asking you to work for the rights and dignities of unborn children. Or you might get involved in some kind of work to prevent unwanted pregnancies. Whatever happens as the result of true intercession, you will not be left unaware of the image of God in that woman, nor of the plight of vulnerable women in society, nor of the rights and needs of unborn children, nor of the plight of people in an overpopulated world.

Focused intercession is hard work. Some people who are called to a life of continuous prayer decide that they can only do this kind of work from inside a cloistered monastery or convent. They devote their whole lives to prayer. They spend much time in intercession. Many monks and nuns choose a relatively few people and issues to pray about in depth. They educate themselves about their chosen subject, watch the news for relevant information, pray most earnestly and then leave any results in God's hands.

Such work is not confined to specialists, however. Many ordinary Christians, who would not think of themselves as experts in prayer, or even as special in any way, are drawn by Christ into this ministry of focused intercession. Those of us who are called to this work are asked to give ourselves to be places where Christ does his reconciling work. So how do we do this? How do we keep fit? How do we avoid getting emotionally overburdened? How do we persevere when our prayers are not answered? How do we manage when we feel that God has been cruel? I suspect the answer to all these questions lies in keeping one's feet on the ground and one's head in heaven!

Practical Ways of Helping Intercessors to Keep Going

We cannot run away from reality. We must face the suffering of our world as it comes to us through the media and through personal contacts with other people. We must be prepared to find God's image in the people who are victims of disasters *and* in the people who cause them. We may have to take a stand for one person, or one side of a contentious issue, but that fact cannot absolve us from the duty of praying for everyone who is involved in that issue. Our own feelings as we carry our petitions to Christ are immaterial. We have to learn to be so attached to Christ that we can allow him to absorb our distress. Our anguish in prayer can become a clean pain that can be offered to Christ as an earnest of our longing for healing.

We must, however, know our own limitations, and not take on too many issues and people at one time. If we are called to focused prayer of the kind I have described, it is unlikely that any one of us will be able to hold more than five people, or issues, in his or her heart at any one time. My own experience has taught me that quite often one person will preoccupy my prayer for days on end. Their needs may wake me in the night. If so, I try to get more rest during the next day. If the burden of prayer is heavy, it is often possible to share it with another person, or with a small group of trusted intercessors, without breaking confidences that must be kept private.

It is my contention that Christians who take the work of intercession seriously do need each other's help. That is what I mean when I say that we need to keep our feet on the ground, even while our heads are in heaven. Otherwise we shall fall into the trap of thinking that *we* are important. We shall swell with pride when others ask us for *our* prayers. We may even attribute beneficial results to *our* intercession. We may even forget always to give God the glory.

If we are to avoid such spiritual pride, we will do well to belong to a prayer group as well as giving time to personal intercession. In such a group we shall come to know that we are but part of the Body of Christ, part of each other, part of his work here on earth. If we belong to a trusted group of people we shall be able to confide in them when we think that we are getting too emotionally involved with someone for whom we are interceding. Our friends may be able to offer wise advice, help us to relax a bit, help us to see another point of view, and occasionally they may be able to lift the burden and carry it for us for a while. Other members of the prayer group will be able to encourage us when we feel weary. In this way, knowing that we do not stand alone, but are part of a great network of prayer, we will stop worrying about the efficacy of *our* prayer. We will be content to have one small share in Christ's work. Above all, we must know, deep down, that it is Christ who is interceding, not us; we must be content to be the space in which he does the work. We must turn to others for help and support, probably more often than we commonly feel able to do.

Intercession, both general and focused, can and frequently does change us. If we persevere, we shall begin to see what God is doing. We shall develop an ability to find Christ in everyone with whom we come into contact. We shall begin to treat other people as if they were made in the image of God. There is an apocryphal story that bears telling again. I do not know its origins, but I have heard it told but twice in the last ten years; this is how it stays with me:

A community was full of people who were constantly in contention with each other. They argued, fought, scrapped over everything. They displayed anger towards each other. Some even hated their companions. When newcomers came and saw what was going on they went away again. The community was dying.

The members of the community were bewildered and saddened. In desperation they prayed. Then, rather surprisingly, they were moved to send for help to an outsider, a local holy man. He came and stayed with them for a while. When he left, he said to them that one of them was the Messiah.

After he had gone the brothers started to ask themselves who the Messiah was. 'Is it Brother John? Or Matthew? Or could it be I?' Since no one knew each began to behave as if his neighbour *was* the Messiah. They greeted each other courteously. They tried to be helpful where help was needed. They began to look on each other with eyes of understanding compassion and love. They began to see the Messiah's reflection in one another.

In time the community was transformed from one where hatred reigned into one where love was paramount. New members came to join. They stayed.[6]

When we can see Christ in everyone we meet through prayer, through the times when 'our head is in heaven', we are half-way to finding the image of God in the people whom we meet in our daily life, when our feet are on the ground. We are half-way to finding their true humanity. Our behaviour towards them will alter: their behaviour towards us may change for the better, or, if they are evil people and discern Christ in us, it will change for the worse. That is part of the joy and the cost of finding the image of God, our true humanity, in ourselves and in others.

CHAPTER 6

SACRED IDLENESS

❧

Surely life is more than food and the body more
than clothing! (Matt. 6: 25)

Certainly work is not always required of man.
There is such a thing as sacred idleness, the culti-
vation of which is now fearfully neglected.
(George MacDonald)[1]

ANDREW ENJOYED his work. He liked nothing better.
When he was fourteen years old he had come across a book
about Abraham Lincoln. In it he was astounded to find these
words attributed to the great man:

My father taught me to work, but not to love it. I never
did like to work, and I don't deny it. I'd rather read, tell
stories, crack jokes, talk, laugh – anything but work.[2]

Andrew couldn't imagine not liking work. He couldn't wait
for the time when he would be old enough to go out to work,
to earn his living, to provide for a family, to achieve success.
He wasn't sure what kind of success he wanted, but sometimes,
at night, when he was by himself, he dreamt of becoming
Archbishop of Canterbury, or a famous and very rich doctor.
Of course, he knew that probably wouldn't happen, but his
ambition fuelled his determination to study.

When Andrew reached university he was pleased to find
himself more intelligent than some of the other students. He
knew he wasn't brilliant, but if hard work combined with a
good intellect could win prizes, that was what he wanted to
do. There was, however, a small price to pay. He had to drop
most of his extra-curricular interests. Instead, he put his head

down and worked. He won his prizes and felt himself to be well set for a good academic career.

Andrew was in his third year when he was converted to Christianity and changed his mind about the kind of career he wanted. He applied to a theological college, was accepted and again found himself doing what he most enjoyed.

He was ordained, served his title at an Anglican church in an inner city area of a provincial city, worked all hours of the day and night and found himself speedily promoted. He had attained the status of vicar before he thought very much about his personal need for companionship. He diverted some of his considerable energies into the search for a wife, married an eminently suitable person and continued his career in the Church. He had warned his bride-to-be, who was a clergyman's daughter, that God came first. He didn't approve of women going out to work. She would have plenty to do at home. After all they would, no doubt, have children, so she wouldn't ever be idle. He 'must be about [his] Father's business'.[3] By that time, having been a vicar for a number of years, he had identified strongly with the person of Jesus Christ, and everyone in the parish, his fiancée included, thought he was a very holy man indeed.

By the age of forty-five Andrew was a successful archdeacon, well on his way to becoming a bishop. If anyone wanted anything done, they asked Andrew. He would hardly ever turn them down. He and Margaret had three children, all doing well at school. He was on umpteen committees and often had to be away for conferences. Margaret looked after him impeccably, so much so that he hardly noticed what she was doing except that he missed her attention dreadfully when she was ill or away to care for her elderly mother. Then he would get petulant, demanding her attention, reminding her that she had left mother, father, family to 'cleave only unto him'.[4]

Andrew was forty-six years old when he had his first heart attack. He nearly died. Afterwards the consultant cardiologist spoke to him in a friendly way. He would need some convalescence, some readjustment to his lifestyle if he was to avoid further heart attacks. Andrew listened, agreed, meant to amend his ways, went home.

He had reckoned without his caring personality, his delight in hard work, his ignorance of what to do with leisure. Within six weeks of his return to work he was living just as he had done before his heart attack. Nothing untoward happened. Margaret worried, of course, nagged him from time to time, fed him more carefully, protected him from all family squabbles, went on loving him in the only way she knew. Andrew began to feel invincible again. After all, as he so often said, *laborare est orare*.[5] 'I enjoy my work. It's my recreation.' Two years later he was appointed a suffragan bishop. He assured his doctors that he had learnt to live with his cardiac condition. He minimised both his symptoms and his overwork. On the eve of his consecration he had another heart attack and died.

Such a story, again a composite story, is not uncommon among caring professionals in countries of the northern hemisphere. Their personalities and lifestyles, together with the expectations of the community they serve, conspire to make a virtue of hard work, even of overwork. When they die prematurely, the world mourns their passing briefly, before transferring the burdens of their office on to the next victim.

It is easy to see the folly of this way of life. The cost of it to the victim's family and colleagues is obvious. The family is impoverished by parental absence. The spouse or partner is starved of companionship. Ultimately, the neglected partner and children sometimes have to cope with a cherished person's total breakdown in health or premature death. The children grow up to repeat the sins of their forebears or, sometimes, to rebel against them in quite antisocial ways.

Someone like Andrew has an effect on his colleagues. Some of them may feel guilty if they don't work as hard as their workaholic associate. Others overwork themselves. A few shrug their shoulders and yet become jealous of their co-worker's apparent success in the eyes of the hierarchy and the world. Some are relieved when their colleague dies.

Society sometimes loses men and women of great talent through their premature deaths, or through disabling illnesses which are the direct result of high stress and overwork.

We live in a world where some men and women do far too much work and others face perpetual unemployment. Some young men and women leaving school will never have paid employment, however much they want it. Others, who do work when they are young, will find themselves redundant in early middle age. Many who do have work will work seven days a week. They are afraid that if they don't comply with their employer's demands they will lose their position. That might not be true: nevertheless the fear is what compels some people to agree to work seven days a week. Some will work until retiring age and then promptly take up another kind of paid employment. Some will work on beyond retiring age, thus preventing a younger person from securing work.

It seems utterly crazy that Western society should be organised in such a way that job supply and demand never match: it means that we are dependent on unemployment, sickness and early deaths to provide work for other people.

It seems equally bizarre that in nearly all Western countries now there is very little sense of the goodness of a community rest day, a sabbath day each week when all work is reduced to a minimum. Yet many of us are too busy getting on with our own lives to sit down and think about possible remedies. 'That's the way society is,' we mutter to ourselves as we continue to collude with the system, and struggle not to lose our own employment. We do not want to have to endure the low status and impoverished lifestyles that we see other people having to put up with.

Even when one does find the time to think, the problems associated with work and leisure seem so great that one scarcely knows where to begin. For Christians the Bible is the obvious place: it is quite clear on the subject. God hallows work because God is creative (Gen. 1—2: 3). God decreed that human beings should earn their living through work (Gen. 3: 17–24). God also helped human beings to see that work could be enjoyable, for even in paradise there is work: 'Yahweh God took the man and settled him in the garden of Eden to cultivate and take care of it' (Gen. 2: 15).

Work is a natural activity. We may rightly expect to be paid for our labour (Luke 10: 7; 1 Tim. 5: 18). Employers are expected to be just, employees to give good measure (Matt. 10: 1–14). Moreover, work can be satisfying as well as materially rewarding because it partakes of God's own activity (John 9: 4). It is pleasing, as St Paul knew (Gal. 6: 1–10).

Throughout history many human beings have found great satisfaction in their work as well as receiving material rewards from it. Others, however, have endured slavery or drudgery for little pleasure or remuneration. Work that partakes of God's creativity is nearly always fulfilling: on the other hand, that which is repetitive and monotonous can be soul-destroying.

This chapter, however, is not concerned with work ethics so much as the distress that human beings bring upon themselves if they do not heed God's laws about rest and recreation. Again the Bible is explicit. God 'rested on the seventh day after all the work he had been doing. God blessed the seventh day and made it holy, because on that day he rested after all his work of creating' (Gen. 2: 3). What seems good to God is good for those created in God's image, and so we find that spelled out in the early chapters of the Bible: the sabbath is sacrosanct (Exod. 23: 10–13; 35: 1–3); work is prohibited on the Day of Atonement (Lev. 16: 29); the land is to lie fallow in the seventh year (Exod. 23: 10); a change of pace is recommended for the sabbath year (Lev. 25: 18–22) and for the year of jubilee which comes every fiftieth year (Lev. 25: 8–17). Jews, Christians and Muslims, all of whom have regard for these chapters of the Old Testament, have good guidelines in the matter of work and rest.

If we really take God's word seriously, we need to heed the principles that lie behind these Mosaic and Levitical prescriptions. While it is true that modern life is so complex that vital services in our world would come to an end were everyone to rest on the same day each week, it is also true that the principle of a rest day every week is very pleasing to God. Moreover, people of all faiths and none enjoy taking time off at weekends. The principle that it is natural to live in a manner that allows work and rest to alternate underlies much of our way of life today. A majority of employers now expect to provide those who work for them with an annual paid holiday, and most people who take holidays thoroughly enjoy them. Some employers now even offer a sabbatical time of leave to their employees.

Christians should be among those who adhere closely to these God-given rhythms of work and rest. A day off each week is not a luxury but a necessity. Like many other Christians I try to witness to my beliefs in God's laws by observing Sunday as a day of rest. If one has to work on Sunday there should be a proper day off on another day. Holidays are important. Sabbaticals during our working lives should be the norm rather than a privilege that relatively few people enjoy.

I cannot say that I have always been a good Christian in respect of finding the right balance between work and rest. I have not been, for there have been times in my life when I have not valued rest and recreation as I should have done. Nevertheless, I do know how I ought to be witnessing to my faith and, on the whole, I do observe the biblical principles. That, however, is not enough, at least it is not enough in today's world. It is, for instance, perfectly possible to replace one's exertions at work with frenetic activity during leisure times. Some people are never still long enough to notice what is happening around them, nor do they notice what is happening to their own bodies and to their families and close friends. They have simply replaced one form of activity with another. Such a change may be enjoyable, even beneficial, but one misses a great opportunity for the 'sacred idleness' of which George MacDonald speaks in the quotation that heads this chapter. Periods of idleness can be truly re-creative and innovative and lead to renewal of energies and new ventures.

The Joys and Benefits of Idleness

In a modern industrialised society relatively few people seem to enjoy doing nothing. If they are encouraged to be idle they tend to feel awkward, useless, inept, inactive, bored. Their minds go on ticking along and, before they know it, they are busy again thinking or worrying about what they're not doing because they are 'sitting down, doing nothing'!

However, it is my belief that 'sacred idleness' is a vital component of a busy life. George MacDonald wrote about it in 1872 when Britain was in the grip of an industrial revolution. His implied criticism of society is still apposite today. Moreover, periods of sacred idleness are needed, not only on Sundays, holidays and religious festivals, but also during each day of our lives.

When I talk about idleness I am not referring to apathy or sloth, both of which were condemned by St Benedict as 'the enemy of the soul'.[6] The kind of idleness I am thinking about is more like that of freewheeling on a bicycle, allowing the vehicle to maintain its own momentum for a space without the rider having to exert any effort to pedal the wheels. If we think of idleness in that way, we will be able to enjoy our rest, knowing that inevitably we will have to start pedalling again after a while.

People who cannot learn that kind of idleness, who, for instance, declare that they have no time to sit down from the moment that get up in the morning to the time they go to bed, are exhausting to be with. They also deplete themselves. Perpetual carers who neglect their own needs are likely to 'burn out', to become so worn out that they suffer a breakdown in health. If they escape that fate they may become so irritable that they are unpleasant to live with.

The ability to be idle is a gift, but it can be caught from others who know that idleness is so restful that it is often succeeded by increased energy and effective work. Indeed, another wise person, Samuel Butler, pointed out that 'to do a great work a man must be very idle as well as very industrious'.[7] How then can we, who are so afraid of being lazy, acquire the habit of idleness, meaning restfulness? Principally, I believe, by what I call 'reflective broodiness'.

In order to explain what I mean by reflective broodiness it is necessary to imagine going for a short walk on a lovely day. At the end of ten minutes one sits down and enjoys the feel of the sun on one's back and allows oneself to drift into a gentle brooding delight. There is no need to think great thoughts about the sun. There is no need to associate the sun's warmth with Christ's love, though that might come as a spontaneous thought. All that is necessary is to experience the delight of being able to feel the sun. Then one gets up and walks back to whatever one was doing before.

There are plenty of other gentle activities that lead into the same kind of peaceful and restful experience: gardening, for instance, or listening to music and then allowing oneself to drift into stillness at the end of the recording. Knitting and calligraphy are other forms of activity that can lead into idleness. One completes a section of knitting, feels the satisfaction in the accomplishment, then stops for a few minutes and enjoys the rest. Or one puts in the intense effort needed for the inscription of a phrase and then pauses to rest. Similarly cleaning the family car, mending an engine, painting a room or putting up some shelves can be so satisfying that one is content to rest for a while after completing the task.

Once we have acquired a little experience through practising these sorts of activity, we are likely to be able to progress to the pure delight of seizing ten minutes alone with a ritual cup of tea or coffee during a busy morning. It is easier to learn about this kind of broody reflection, or recreation, when we are alone, but in time it can be done with other people, particularly if they are restful people who are content to be silent.

Initially, it will be a fight to get the time we need to learn to do nothing, to freewheel as it were. Most of us are so habituated to sequential activity that we feel guilty when we begin, but once we have experienced the benefits of idleness we will not easily surrender them to our superegos that demand that we always should be busy.

I do not speak like this because I am retired and have plenty of time at my disposal. Like many other people, I have found retirement poses its own problems about the use of time. Being free, either because of long-term unemployment or retirement, means that other people frequently make demands which they think one should be able to fulfil because 'you don't go out to work'. It is just as difficult for retired and habitually unemployed people to find the time to be idle as it is for those who are gainfully employed.

Certainly, I find I have no more time at my disposal now than I did when I was a busy general medical practitioner. It was, indeed, during those years that I first learnt to be idle. At that time of my life people often asked me where my energy and capacity for doing several things at one time came from, and

I would reply truthfully that they came from my ability to be idle at frequent intervals. When someone can control their daily timetable, as I can, this is easy to do. It is not nearly so easy to do if you are on a factory production line, if you are trying to care for three small children or elderly parents, or are part of a team at work, or perhaps bound by a rigid routine as one sometimes is in a hospital, prison or convent. In those circumstances a tea break or going to the toilet are the only ways one can get the space for recreational idleness. Nevertheless, even for employees, work does come to an end and the first thing one should do on returning home is to find time to sit down and rest for a few minutes. Even demanding spouses and children can be encouraged to give the wage-earner this space.

I have previously referred to focused attention on a memory of a peaceful place as a way of entering silence. This method can also be used for periods of brief rest during each day, but they cannot, I think, wholly replace our need for periodic idleness. Some people, however, have developed this art of reaching a resting state to a fine point. It is said that Wellington could 'sleep on his feet'. Much the same account is given of Rab Butler: he could sit through a complex discussion in committee, appearing to be asleep. After a while, he would suddenly revive and sum up the proceedings with incredible clarity. His 'empty' mind had absorbed and analysed all that he had heard during his period of restful broodiness.

Some people can undoubtedly learn to do what came naturally to Wellington and Rab Butler, by a simple relaxation technique. Electroencephalographic recordings of brain rhythms have shown that alert resting states are accompanied by the appearance of alpha waves in the recordings. Using a simple feedback brain-conditioning technique most people can be trained to produce these alpha waves at will. When they appear the subject feels at rest and comes back into full activity greatly refreshed. This is, then, yet another way of learning deep relaxation.[8]

Some people want to learn this kind of broody restfulness but they find it difficult to do so by themselves. There are many courses available now that help one to acquire the art.

Transcendental meditation is the most widely known and used relaxation technique in the West, but there is an increased interest among Christians in Zen meditation and in Buddhist methods of attaining inner peace.[9]

I have not counted times of prayer or retreat as times of sacred idleness, because in my experience they can be hard work, but whenever I am in retreat for several days I do find it beneficial to stop whatever I am thinking or doing from time to time to enjoy resting. If we are tired we are likely to go to sleep, but then that too is God's way of enabling us to rest prior to and after activity. Catnaps can be very recreational.

The best kind of rest is when we are not tired but alert and capable of being totally relaxed. It is also possible in those circumstances to spend several hours just sitting, and this too can be helpful. People often report that they return from these periods refreshed and recharged with energy. Often the solution to a particular problem will present itself to them in the hours immediately following such a period of sacred idleness. Sometimes rest is followed by a period of intense creativity.

So far I have spoken about idleness as reflective broodiness, a kind of freewheeling as if one were on a bicycle, and have associated it with physical rest, or absence of external activity. I have focused on this form of idleness because I feel it is important to acquire this skill if one can and it is so often neglected. There are, however, people who cannot ever feel happy sitting down and doing nothing. If they try to do that they just get more and more tense, irritable and restless. These people need to use rhythmic physical activity to absorb surface energy sufficiently to allow their minds to freewheel. It seems that long-distance swimming, rambling, hill-walking, jogging, 'dancing in the spirit',[10] 'tai chi',[11] circle dancing[12] and aerobics are all helpful activities that allow one's mind to rest while one's body is absorbed in movement. Some people would say that they can ride a horse or a bicycle, or drive a car, and get the same kind of effect, but I would question the wisdom of trying to achieve mental rest while pursuing an activity which may require instantly refocused concentration if one is to avoid disaster.

Western society has lost its way in regard to work and rest.

It understands about work and play, but not work and rest. This is one of the areas where the example of Christians is sorely needed. Christians can do much by example to promote the goodness of true idleness. They can observe the sabbath as an opportunity for pleasurable rest. This is not, as in some former times, to be seen as an invitation to boredom, a restriction on all enjoyable activity, but as a time when one refrains from work and Sunday shopping, and spends at least some time during the day 'putting one's feet up', doing nothing. Christians can also do a lot by example by taking shorter periods of rest during each day in an obvious manner. If they learn to do that they will also learn that they can control time rather than having to allow themselves to be controlled by time. After all, did not our Lord command us to 'look at the birds in the sky' (Matt. 6: 27), and to 'think of the flowers in the field' (Matt. 6: 28). If we truly trust God, and set our hearts on God's Kingdom first, 'and on God's saving justice' (Matt. 6: 33), everything else will fall into place in God's good time.

CHAPTER 7

THE DELIGHT OF REVERENCE

❦

*We have been given possession of an unshakeable king-
dom. Let us therefore be grateful and use our gratitude
to worship God in the way that pleases him, in reverence and fear. For our God is a consuming fire. (Heb.
12: 28–9)*

*I do wish there was more reverence in our everyday
life. We would be the richer for it, whether it be for
nature, work or people.* (William Sykes)[1]

AGNES WAS fourteen when she discovered she had a problem.
She was fat: not just plump, fat. Agnes only discovered that she
had this problem when she went to the school doctor for a
routine medical examination. Before that day, she had known
that she was large. All her family were well built. She had
assumed that some people were made that way from the beginning. After all her best friend was as thin as a rake and could
eat anything she liked without putting on a pound. If Agnes
ate a currant bun it would turn itself straight into an extra
dollop of fat beneath her skin.

The doctor was middle-aged and decidedly scrawny: her
tone as she addressed the shy young woman was one of hardly
disguised disgust.

'You're too heavy. You'll be dead by the time you're thirty
if you don't stop being so greedy.'

Agnes had been well trained by her mother. She smiled
politely and said nothing. This seemed to inflame the doctor.
Perhaps she had spent the morning struggling with a headache.

'You don't seem to understand. Obesity it a dangerous disease. It can lead to high blood pressure, heart disease, diabetes,
all kinds of problems. Besides,' she added, 'you'll never get a

man to marry you, looking like you do!' She had played her
trump card.

She turned away from the silent young woman before her.
'I'll see you in six months. Make sure you've done something
about it by then. Nurse will help you. Bye now.'

Nurse was a large woman, too. She smiled sympathetically
as Agnes went out of the room. Agnes went straight to the
school tuck shop, bought two buns and consumed them rapidly.
Then she went to the lavatory and cried.

Agnes kept her problem. She became self-conscious. She
despised herself and began to neglect the care of her body.
Although she said nothing at home, she always found an excuse
to be off sick when the doctor came to her school.

When she was sixteen, she managed to attract the attentions
of an equally large youth. When she lost her virginity she felt
triumphant, not because she had enjoyed intercourse, but
because she had proved the school doctor wrong.

It would be good to say that Agnes lived 'happily ever after',
but she didn't. By the time she came to see me some years
later she was still obese and still absolutely miserable about it.
She had, as she said, 'tried everything and nothing had
worked'. She was married to her large partner, but they were
childless. She looked dowdy. Her hair was mousey. She sat
slumped in her chair as if to try to hide her size from me. Her
self-esteem was very low. Agnes was convinced that she was
being punished by God for greediness.

'You are not greedy, Agnes,' I said, after I had listened to her
story. 'You might have a compulsive eating disorder, but you
are *not* greedy. You do binge from time to time, but you're not
able to stop. You'd only be guilty of greed if you could control
your eating habits and deliberately decided to overindulge. Let's
try to find out what is happening and see if you can help
yourself to treat your body with the reverence it deserves.'

Agnes was never put on a formal diet. Instead she and her
husband were invited to talk about their feelings about their
childlessness.

Today Agnes could not be described as thin, but she is not
fat either. The couple do not have any children of their own,
but they are splendid houseparents in a residential home for

young people with behaviour disorders. They are happy and fulfilled.

Agnes' story shows us how easy it is to judge people by their appearance. It proves the wisdom of looking beneath the surface to the person who is struggling to express his or her needs. It shows that one may help men and women to find healing without necessarily immediately attending to their presenting symptoms.

There is one other factor in Agnes' case history that so far has not emerged in my account. We live in a society which exploits people's weaknesses and vulnerabilities. In such a society people can be persuaded by skilled advertising to be greedy for experience. Agnes was carried away by the anticipatory pleasure of eating the foods she saw on television advertisements and in supermarket store promotions and so she sometimes bought products she did not really need.

In any industrial society based on what is called a 'free market', manufacturers have to persuade consumers to buy their products, although these may be harmful to some of those who will purchase them. Heavy advertising campaigns tempt us to want what we see and hear about. They play to our weaknesses by making us believe that we are strong enough to make sensible use of the goods we buy. I have already discussed some of the ill effects of living in a consumer society (see pp. 49ff.), but in this chapter I am more concerned with our collective greed for sensual experience of all kinds.

In Western society most people who are alive today will have been exposed to the public portrayal of sensual experience through fantasy situations. This takes place chiefly through the media. Exposure to situations where the emotions are stimulated starts at an early age, often when the radio or television set is left on during periods of the day when the infants or children of the household appear to be taking no notice of what is going on around them. Their emotional responses to these stimuli may go unnoticed, but they remain dormant in their memories and can be revived and reinforced at a later age by repeated stimulation. This means that many adults are unaware of the extent to which they are vulnerable to advertising which makes use of overt or covert subliminal techniques which appeal to their sensual natures.

None of us are untouched by such appeals. We all have some weaknesses in this respect. Sometimes, as with food and drugs, we can buy a sensual experience. Often, however, as with sexual or quasi-mystical experience, we do not need to buy it. We can get a taste for it by watching television or reading the newspapers and magazines. We can be titillated by what we are seeing and then, given the right circumstances, we may be tempted to take whatever it is that we want, at other people's expense if necessary.

During their search for sensual experience some people may induce others to join them. There are, for instance, some people who play out their sadomasochistic fantasies by looking at pornographic material. Unfortunately, a few may go on to play out their sexual and/or violent fantasies with, or against, real human beings. In extreme cases activists can persuade others to become members of an unsavoury pornographic ring or a group that indulges in cruelty for its kicks. Similarly, young adults may join in a quasi-religious cult only to find themselves dominated by older people who are using their superior strength and intellectual cunning to force their desires on to those who are physically weaker and/or emotionally vulnerable. There are cults that make use of drugs to heighten quasi-mystical experience. There are others that attract new members because they offer the delights of sensual bodily and religious experience in a mutually supportive closed community. People who are attracted to such rings and cults are often fragile men and women. They may be very damaged by their experiences, especially if they do not have the mental strength to withdraw from membership before they become brainwashed by the leaders.

The examples quoted here are extreme, but other less obvious ways of appealing to our collective greed for sensual experience also do considerable damage.

As well as living in a consumer society we also live in an acquisitive one. What one person has, others often want. They not only want it: when they get it, they want more and more. They become greedy for the experience. They sometimes get it at a cost that they should not be paying. Some people, for instance, may daydream about winning the pools or the National Lottery. They feed their excitement by gambling money they haven't got. Other people may dream about becoming football stars or successful actors. Unfortunately their talent doesn't match their aspirations: they may take out their frustrations in antisocial behaviour that is damaging to the people they meet in real life.

Those of us who think that we are immune from greed for food and sex or other forms of dependency on sensual experience are often deluded. Most of us can be seduced into one form of acquisitiveness or another by subtle temptations. Some of us may look disdainfully on those who are greedy for excitement. We think that we stand above these forms of greed. However, we may compensate for what we have missed by buying into some other form of excitement.

Analytical observation of the current situation within denominational Churches suggests that greed for experience is a phenomenon that exists in all sections of the Christian community. Some quite religious people, for instance, may look for the ecstasy of mystical experience, even if it means using hallucinogenic drugs as a short cut.[2] It is, however, not necessary to use drugs at all. When, for instance, people go to charismatic worship services they are sincere: some may be hoping for baptism in the Holy Spirit. Many do have a genuine religious experience. Yet, almost without knowing it, some of them enjoy their religious experience so much that they go on seeking to repeat the experience rather than being content with what they have been given on one occasion. There is, admittedly, a fine line between an authentic experience of the Holy Spirit and a self-induced state of excitement. Often it will only be the fruits of the experience that will distinguish the one from the other (cf. Matt. 7: 16–20).

Most religious leaders are people of great integrity and sincerity. In a few instances, however, they become addicted to their status as trendsetters, preachers or healers. Their disciples may collude with their addiction and boost their need for adulation by following them to the point of hysteria.

Even if we don't go to those extremes we may slip into

another form of greed for experience. One form of spirituality, for instance, becomes fashionable among Christians. Books and workshops about it multiply. Authors, teachers and enthusiasts proliferate. Many people earn a good living from the spirituality that is currently 'all the rage'. In time, however, interest in that particular form of devotion may wane. Its popularity subsides: another kind of spirituality comes to take its place and the whole cycle begins again. In the last fifty years we have seen fluctuations in the fortunes of Benedictine spirituality, Ignatian contemplation, Celtic mysticism, transcendental meditation, creationism and New Age spirituality, to mention but a few popular movements that have preoccupied the time and energies of many relatively affluent Western Christians. In themselves they may be good but, taken to excess, they divert attention from the crying needs of today's world.

All these temptations surround us today and it is easy to succumb. We see someone else having an experience we think we need. We put ourselves in the way of getting it for ourselves. By the time we have obtained it, the fashion may have changed, so we set off in hot pursuit of the next experience or excitement. Nevertheless, paradoxically, it is within this search for sensual experience that the cure of its greedy aspects is to be found. We can find our healing by learning to greet each moment of experience with reverence.

The Significance of the Present Moment

Many Christians are familiar with Brother Lawrence's classic, *The Practice of the Presence of God*.[3] This seventeenth-century Carmelite lay brother found God in all the tiny events and actions of each day. He savoured each moment of the day because he used it as an opportunity to become aware of God's presence. He found that time and eternity collide in the present moment. He tried to live in that moment. Many present-day Christians still find his writings helpful. They too try to become aware of God in the everyday events of life and sometimes even refer to 'the sacrament of the present moment', meaning that each moment of time is the outward and visible sign of the inward presence of God with us all the time.

In speaking about reverence for the present moment, however, I am not using that term in exactly the same way as Brother Lawrence did. Instead, I am thinking about being able to reside in a moment and to enjoy it to the full without wanting to hold on to it, without lamentation for the past or undue eagerness for the future. This way of using time is a necessary precursor to becoming aware of God's presence at all times and in all places, as I shall hope to show later in this chapter.

By way of illustration let me describe what once happened to a young man called Jeff, who set out to climb a small mountain. He had never done this particular ascent before, but he had considerable experience of rock-climbing and he knew that he was competent to tackle this test of skill and courage alone. He wanted to get to the top. He wanted to see the surrounding countryside from the vantage point of the summit. Jeff had known that kind of pleasure before and he was looking for it again. Among his motives for the climb there were two that were important to him: he wanted to prove that he was physically fit; he was also aware that he knew fear every time he climbed in dangerous terrain and he wanted to challenge that emotion in himself.

As Jeff stood at the bottom of the mountain, he told me later, he knew that he wanted the elation that comes from completing what one sets out to do: he intended to reach the summit. At that moment he was conscious of a strong feeling of well-being. He felt fit. The sun was up, the weather forecast favourable, the wind light. His gear was in good shape. He set off.

The peak of the mountain cannot be seen from its lower reaches, so he concentrated on the immediate task of feeling his way up the rocks that lay ahead. He liked the challenge, the careful positioning of his feet, the belays, the struggle to get past an overhanging rock. He enjoyed his rest periods, the splendid views, the feel of the breeze on his face, the satisfaction of finding a handhold in what looked like a smooth sheet of stone.

Several hours passed. As Jeff neared his goal he realised that the weather was closing in on him. It had taken more time than he had anticipated to get so far, and it was getting cold. If he went on, he would probably have to bivouac in bad weather conditions on the way down, for night would come before he could get right off the mountain. For a few minutes he considered doing that: he was, as always, equipped for such emergencies. Looking up, he saw the summit. It looked so close: in reality there was another thousand feet of difficult terrain between him and the top.

Some mountaineers would have gone on: some might have reached their goal. Jeff decided that he had enjoyed the day so much that he didn't need to spoil it by risking disaster. He turned back and came off the mountain. It would still be there next year. It was, and this time he reached the pinnacle; it was a satisfying experience.

The point of this story is to suggest that in attending to the moment of truth when he faced the reality of the bad weather Jeff had acted wisely, not only for himself, but also for those who might have had to mount a rescue bid. Some time afterwards he told me that he had learnt a spiritual lesson from his climb that he would never have done had he stayed at the bottom of the mountain, or got to the top on that first try. He had learnt to have a deep respect for the journey itself as opposed to the task and the goal.

'It almost amounted to reverence for the experience I was having,' he said. 'I didn't need anything more!'

This young man's experience was fascinating, but it also had meaning beyond the obvious one. For that sense of awe that one sometimes has for a particular moment, a particular phase of one's life, has its parallels in the spiritual journey of prayer.

Prayer is a bit like climbing a mountain. The goal, the mountain-top, as it were, is union with God. In order to undertake it we need to be fit, well trained and equipped. At the outset most of us realise that we are not going to get to the summit in one swift dash. Although we know that there are people like St Paul, for instance, who are taken into the third heaven for God's purposes (2 Cor. 12: 2), we also know that we are unlikely to be among those to whom this happens. We might, of course, try to take a short cut. We could fly to the summit, land by helicopter, or get there by mountain railway or chairlift.[4] Such a passive method of transport will not give us the same experience, either on the journey or at the summit, as we would have were we to climb.

Few people who enjoy walking or hill-climbing want to be air-lifted to the top. They enjoy the journey. So it is with those of us who are Christian pilgrims. Many of us are content to walk the journey, knowing that God may carry us only a little way up the mountain before we are set down on our own two feet and invited to follow Jesus for the rest of the way. Moreover, however well we know the route, however many times we have climbed a particular mountain, each time is new, each time teaches us something we did not know before, and when we get to the summit we will see other mountains to climb that will bring us still closer to God. For as long as we live we shall need to go on climbing, yet paradoxically we shall also find God on the descents into the valleys that, in their own way, are as beautiful and awesome as the hills.

It will be on this slow journey towards our ultimate destination that we shall learn to reverence the present moment of experience. It comes through ordinary and joyous events in time: the sight of a new bud in spring, the lifting of the heart at the sound of a newborn first grandchild, the sigh of relief in a father's heart when he looks at his new daughter, the thankfulness that one can still get angry at injustice, the unexpected moments when Love is disclosed: these are all moments in time to be savoured and remembered.

Reverence for the present moment also comes through the starkness of the events that bring us suffering: the day when someone dear to us falls and breaks her leg, the awful toothache in the middle of the night, the phone call that brings the bad news that mother is dying from cancer, the day the dog has to be put down, the sight of a manager's eyes as he dismisses a colleague, the fear that one might be next in line; these are moments that bring us to our knees. They are points that we pass on our journey to God, yet they are moments that make our lives significant, far more significant than our possessions, status or physical environment.

If we are to savour the journey itself, if we are to bring memories of the past into our present experience and to

embrace them in the present moment, we will have to let go
of a temptation to live in either the past or the future. This
kind of letting go is exciting. Each day brings its own rewards
and pains. Each day is a challenge. We do not have to buy
ecstasy or take care to avoid pain. They are part of the journey.
They enable us to travel hopefully. In a curious way these
moments, where we are humbled by joy or by suffering, make
hardship, pain, disillusionment, darkness and aridity in prayer,
monotony and tedium at work bearable as nothing else does.
This will, however, happen only if we embrace these moments
rather than trying to avoid them by pretending to be detached
from all sensual stimuli.

Practical Ways of Learning to Enjoy and Revere the Present Moment

If we want to learn to enjoy the present moment, our present
situation, the rhythm of our ordinary lives we have to learn to
be observant. Now this is a reversal of the kind of spiritual
advice that formerly used to be given to people, like myself,
who wanted to learn to pray continuously.

When I started out on my Christian pilgrimage at the age
of eighteen, I was encouraged to detach myself from every
kind of sensual experience. Such advice led me to misuse
Brother Lawrence's wise sayings by trying not to notice what
was happening around me. Instead, I tried to focus my mind
on the transcendence of God. I also tried to ignore anything
that might arouse my bodily and emotional senses. I was
remarkably good at it: I could walk for miles without noticing
anything that was there before my feet; I knew how to sit in
the middle of a crowd and not listen to anything that was said;
I became indifferent to what I was eating or drinking. The
advice I received from my elders had a purpose. It *was* a kind
of protest against materialism, egoism, greed for experience.
Unfortunately, in the early stages starvation often heightens the
senses and increases the appetite. Paradoxically, it is only after
prolonged starvation that one ceases to want to eat or enjoy
other kinds of sensual experience. So I did what many other
people still do. I moved like a pendulum between sensual

starvation and satiation, became despondent about my weaknesses and unmoved by relative success.

It took me years to learn to change my ways. I wish now that some kind spiritual director had taken me by the scruff of the neck, shaken me, and made me learn to look at everything, and everyone, with reverence. As it was, I had to learn that lesson by myself, slowly and painfully. In the end it was forced on me because the way of detachment, in its false guise of sensual starvation and emotional separation from everything 'other than God', failed to help me to grow more attached to God and more compassionate towards my companions.

I was fortunate enough to come upon a book that set me on a better road: it was Archbishop Anthony Bloom's *School for Prayer*; it helped me greatly in many ways, especially to find the presence of God in ordinary places, people, events and moments of time. I listened to the advice that Archbishop Bloom once gave to a woman who had been trying to perceive God's presence for fourteen years and failed to do so. He advised her:

> Go to your room, after breakfast, put it right, place your armchair in a strategic position, . . . just sit, look round, and try to see where you live, because I am sure that if you have prayed all these fourteen years it is a long time since you have seen your room. And then take your knitting and for fifteen minutes knit before the face of God, but I forbid you to say one word of prayer. You just knit and try to enjoy the peace of your room.[5]

I too followed that advice and, like Archbishop Anthony's old lady, found that I noticed things about the room that I had never noticed before. I also saw how peaceful the room felt and, for the first time, how full of 'presence' it felt, presence that made me feel happy and in tune with my room and, after a while, with the people who came into my thoughts. That was the beginning of a change in my attitudes. In time I became more observant of everything in my surroundings. I began to see them in relation to God and I began to find God within them, and them in God.

I stopped being greedy for what I hadn't got because I had

been given so much delight in each moment. Like many other Christians I also found myself full of reverence for the things I was receiving from God's hands each day. This reverence has grown. It springs from a perception that everything we are given comes from God. When we understand, see and experience that we are well on the way to learning to worship God through finding God's transcendence within the immanent moments of each day.

There are, of course, many other ways of learning this way of resisting greed through finding our true fulfilment. If one goes to a Franciscan house anywhere in the world one will find people living very simply and poorly, yet they are often full of joy that overflows. The same can be said of the Little Brothers and Sisters of Jesus.[6] They have discovered this gift of being poor, yet rich in spirit. They can accept the good things of life that are given to them, but they also bless God when they are deprived of things that they need. We can learn from them and acquire the gift of true simplicity that frees one from cupidity of all kinds.

Perhaps the greatest antidote to a greedy desire for sensual gratification comes from the realisation that one is mortal. Once we realise that we are going to die our attitude towards present experience changes, often quite dramatically. For instance, as soon as we knew that my husband was going to die our attitude towards material goods and future pleasures altered. We stopped thinking about what we might have, or do, in the future because there wasn't going to be one. Yet our pleasure in the good things that happened during each day increased. Suddenly, we realised that we might never 'pass this way again'. Meeting friends became precious. We could not waste our time together. We talked about things that mattered greatly. When we were alone we communed with each other in warm shared silences that conveyed our feelings better than words could have done. Neither of us waited for our birthdays if we wanted to give small tokens of affection to each other.

Small moments of each day became etched on my memory as they came and went. I can still feel what I felt one day when I was watching our old mongrel dog nestling up to my husband's knee. Outings to places we loved became intensely enjoyable.

We learned to live every day as if it were our last together, but also to live as if we were going to go on for ever. We began to see what was important to us and what was not. Living in this 'end time' lasted for several months before he died. There were many bad days as well as good days, but on most days we found some moments of delight. He left me a rich legacy, for I have gone on living in 'end time' ever since, though I am not yet as close to death, perhaps, as he was when we discovered this way of living.

The realisation that we are mortal is a gift, a gift we often seem to try to refuse, yet one that, when we accept it, transforms our attitudes towards material goods, greed for sensual experience and 'tomorrow', for, as the author of James' letter to the twelve tribes of the dispersion says, 'you never know what will happen tomorrow' (Jas. 4: 14), and as Luke says, 'you too must stand ready, because the Son of man is coming at an hour you do not expect' (Luke 12: 40).

As Christians we know that we are mortal. We believe in our resurrection from the dead. Our hope is in God. So we should have the kind of strength that can stand against greed, without being judgemental on other people. We can enjoy each moment as it comes to us, even if it seems harsh or painful. By faith, we believe that we are living in end time and so we should be able to live in ways that are consistent with that knowledge that our treasure is in heaven. Our many failures cannot excuse us from this kind of witness, but the rewards of success are great, not only for ourselves but for those who catch God's meaning.

CHAPTER 8

THE MUSIC OF SILENCE

⁊⁊

*But Yahweh is in his holy Temple: let the whole earth
be silent before him.* (Hab. 2: 20)

*Elected silence sing to me
And beat upon my whorlèd ear,
Pipe me to pastures still and be
The music that I care to hear.*
(Gerard Manley Hopkins,
'The Habit of Perfection')

JEREMY ENJOYED the Sunday morning Eucharists at his
local Anglican church, but he found himself irritated by one
part of the service.

After the sermon, the vicar would come back to his place,
sit down and keep silence for about a minute, sometimes two
minutes. Jeremy noticed that the whole congregation fell into
a holy hush. Sometimes, but not often, the silence was broken
by a baby crying. On occasion, one or two people coughed or
sneezed. This embarrassed Jeremy as much as it did them.
Once, to his horror, an old tramp who had strayed into the
back of the church seeking warmth shouted an obscenity during
the silence. He was quickly removed by the churchwardens.

Jeremy was always pleased when the vicar got up and the
singing started again: but then the whole performance was
repeated when everyone had returned to their places after
receiving Holy Communion. He couldn't understand it at all.

'I don't know what to do,' he said to the churchwarden one
Sunday morning after church.

'You can't settle to anything: I never know when it's going
to end; besides it feels like an interruption. Why can't the vicar
get on with it?'

'He's trying to help us to think about what we've just heard and done,' Angela said, and added, 'Does silence scare you?'

'Of course not!' he laughed.

The conversation ended there. They moved away to talk to other friends in the congregation.

Jeremy felt uncomfortable. Had he asked a silly question? Why did he still feel uneasy? He drank his coffee quickly, and went home. He loved his house: it had been his home for the last twenty years. He had retired early to look after his ailing wife during the last years of her life. After her death his daughters had urged him to move closer to them, but he had resisted their pleas. Now, a year later, he felt he had adjusted well.

When he got home he went straight to the kitchen and turned on the radio to listen to one of his favourite programmes as he prepared lunch. After his meal he settled down in front of the television. This was how he always spent Sunday afternoons. He liked being on his own that day. It was the one day on which he didn't have to meet people, flatter them, persuade them to buy the goods he sold to make his living.

He had just tuned in to the football match when the power cut came. Jeremy swore. He had wanted to see that game. He got up and went to fetch the radio. It was then that he thought of Angela's question and his reply. He stopped. Of course he wasn't afraid of silence; or was he?

He left the radio off and began to think about it. He had always thought that he liked silence. Certainly he disliked too much noise. He hated the sound of aeroplanes flying across his house in the early hours of the morning. He could understand the outcry of people who felt that their houses would be devalued if a proposed motorway was to come too near to their street. He could also sympathise with men and women who had to work all day long in a noisy factory where you could scarcely hear yourself speak.

On occasion, especially when it had been a hard day at work, Jeremy felt tired out by the sound of customers' voices. When the Sunday trading laws had altered, he had refused to work on Sundays for several reasons, including that one. He didn't need the extra money now that Beth was dead and the children had left home. Besides, being a Christian, he felt rather good about not working on the Lord's day of rest. As for TVs, hi-fi, tape recorders and radios blaring all day long through his neighbours' windows, well he was the first to go round and tell those inconsiderate wretches to turn the volume down.

'Too much noise', Jeremy thought to himself, 'can be exhausting. Certainly it's tiring if it's unpleasant noise, in the wrong place or at the wrong time.'

He remembered Angela's question: 'Are you afraid of silence?'

'Of course not!'

He loved going for walks in the country where it was so quiet and you could listen to the sounds of nature. He enjoyed being in a quiet church for a few minutes of prayer. Where else was it quiet? Nowhere! Except, he supposed, in the church service, but that was a peculiar and unnatural silence wasn't it? Anything as deliberate as that must be.

He realised that, for the first time in many weeks, he was sitting in a silent room on a Sunday afternoon. It was slightly unnerving. The absence of sound didn't feel companionable. He was left alone with the sound of his own thoughts. If he went on like this he'd get morbid. He might even have to think about Angela's question a bit more.

Suddenly a memory hit him like a sledgehammer. He recalled the terrible moment that Beth had stopped breathing. She had been taken ill in the night. He had rung the doctor. By this time she was unconscious, but as he waited he listened to the dreadful but reassuring sound of her laboured breathing. Then, several minutes before the doctor arrived, there was nothing. Nothing. Afterwards, when the doctor had gone, he had spent the night alone. He had not wanted to ring his daughters until the morning. It had been a horrible night.

He got up and turned the radio on.

Jeremy had arrived at an understanding of why a certain kind of silence, dead silence, felt uneasy.

'I haven't got over Beth's death,' he said to himself, 'or perhaps I am afraid of my own death.'

A few days later he acknowledged both fears and went to see the vicar because he had realised that he needed help.

We can leave Jeremy's story there. It illustrates several issues about noise, both its benefits and its disadvantages.

The Benefits of Noise

All of us are thankful for pleasant sounds. Music, the sound of church bells, birdsong, a cat purring, kindly speech, soft words, the reassuring click of a key turning in a lock as one's beloved partner comes home, the grunt of ecstasy during lovemaking, the sound of a newborn child's first cry, the noise of cooking when one is hungry are all sounds that are wonderful to hear. Pleasant sounds like those can bring us great happiness.

There are occasions when noise is preferable to silence. The majority of people in the northern hemisphere live in towns. Being used to noise, they find it reassuring. They prefer pleasant noise to cacophony, and so they deliberately manufacture pleasing sounds to blot out unpleasant noises, thoughts and feelings. So it is common to find music, or the radio, playing in homes, factories, dentists' waiting-rooms and surgeries, hospital wards and some shops. Such sounds can be a welcome distraction from the boredom of housework, unwanted thoughts, loneliness, fear. Then, too, voices can be comforting when we are recovering from an anaesthetic, frightened, grief-stricken; they are reassuring in unfamiliar situations of all kinds. They can be therapeutic too. When, like Jeremy, we cannot face the ultimate silence of bodily death many of us need comforting sounds as balm to our grief.

There are other situations, too, where speech is preferable to silence. If, for instance, two lovers, partners or work colleagues are having a tiff an angry silence can be destructive. In those circumstances a joke that generates laughter may break up the vicious atmosphere.

Sometimes we do not like the noises that we hear but we need them to warn us of impending danger, so we are grateful, for instance, for the cry of a baby in pain, the warning scream that tells us of an approaching car, the screech of brakes, the sounds of an intruder at the door.

There are some circumstances, too, when speech is highly appropriate: if, for instance, someone is being unjustly attacked and one says nothing, one may do positive harm. It would be far better to speak out, even to cry out, on behalf of the victim than to stay silent.

Pleasant or therapeutic noises, sounds and words are not detrimental to the health and happiness of people, indeed of all created beings. We do, however, need to be aware of the potential hazards of unpleasant sounds.

The Disadvantages of Noise

In Western society continuous background noise is common in a big city or town. People become accustomed to it. They only notice it when it is absent, or misplaced, or unduly unpleasant. Otherwise, they tend to ignore it.

The absence of background noise can be quite unpleasant when you are not used to it. It leaves you with your own thoughts. It can prevent you from sleeping. Indeed, some townspeople do not like spending holidays in the countryside or at the seaside because the quiet is so unfamiliar. Whenever they go to the countryside, they will either take some manufactured noise with them, or go to a place where they can have the best of both worlds from their point of view – the countryside or seaside by day, and good entertainment by night.

Such attitudes towards noise are less prevalent in the countryside, where many people's work takes them out into the fields, and where villages are relatively quiet for much of the day and all the night. The introduction of manufactured noise, in the shape of television and all kinds of audio-equipment, has, however, meant that many people in the countryside are also becoming seduced away from silence by music and radio chatter, without fully realising what is happening to them in consequence.

There are physical effects of noise that are quite harmful to human beings. If we have to work in a very noisy environment, or spend our days listening to loud sounds coming through headphones, we may suffer from hearing loss prematurely.

When we work against a background of noise, we have to spend some energy ignoring it, or thinking through it. This means that we get tired. It also means that we may have a lapse of concentration: consequently, our minds may stray towards what we are hearing, yet trying to ignore; then we may have an accident. Our general ability to think coherently may also be impaired by continuous background noise: on the other hand, it appears that some people have now become so accustomed to it that they find they achieve better results if they have the radio or music on while they are working. Many people become irritable through living and working in a crowded environment with a high level of background noise. This is not always appreciated by employers, who cram people into crowded open-plan offices.

Then, too, the distractions of noise can be seductive. They enable us to avoid thoughts and feelings towards which we should be attentive. If we leave those thoughts and feelings submerged, either deliberately or because we are unaware of their existence, they will accumulate until they erupt unexpectedly, sometimes uncomfortably, as they did with Jeremy.

The levels of background noise are now so high and noise is so continuous that it is difficult to appreciate just how damaging all this noise can be. In recent years, however, there has been a welcome rebellion against noise pollution and a deeper appreciation of the value of silence.

The Harmonies of Silence

Many people are looking for places where they can enjoy being quiet: sometimes they just want to enjoy a restful silence, sometimes to reflect on their lives without interruption. Some folk take themselves into the countryside, 'away from it all', for a day out or an afternoon's excursion. Others deliberately choose to visit lonely places for their annual holidays. During their working week some men and women seek refuge in the quiet and prayerful atmosphere of a church, though unfortunately many churches are now shut during the week because of vandalism. Others are open, but filled with noise and bustle. Convents, monasteries and retreat houses, which specialise in providing places where guests can find a quiet and restful atmosphere, are well used, not only by Christian people but also by those of other faiths or none. Small Christian hotels and 'quiet homes' are providing nourishment for many people.

Couples may choose to spend much of their leisure time in a companionable silence, spending their evenings by a fire in a quietness that is friendly and restful. Single people often tell me how much they appreciate the freedom they have to live in quiet homes, to turn off their radios and televisions whenever they want to do so. In hospitals and residential homes for people needing care, there are some ill and elderly people who request that the ward television or 'canned' music be turned off so that they can be quiet, or 'can hear themselves think'.

The presence of periods of warm and harmonious silence in people's lives may be beneficial and restful, even to the point where it can be called, as Gerard Manley Hopkins puts it, 'music that I care to hear'. To think of silence in this way is, however, not enough. We have to ask ourselves what silence is for.

There are, I believe, many answers to that question. The first, and most obvious one, has already been alluded to, because it is the one that we nearly all long for and some of us can enjoy, namely the restful aspect of silence.

Silence can also be creative in that insights and inspirational thoughts often come to people during times when they are alone and quiet. Silence enables them to hear the 'still small voice', 'the light murmuring sound' of God (1 Kgs. 19: 12). Out of that encounter come words of life, thoughts that are meant to be used, words that are given by the Holy Spirit to be said, good actions that are done. Such experiences do not necessarily come only to Christians: for instance, they abound in the experiences of the Old Testament leaders and prophets.[1] Christians believe that all inspiration, all human creativity, all good deeds are inspired by God. It is this aspect of silence that is so important and that is so badly needed in our noise-filled industrialised world.

Silence begets awe, the kind of adoration of which Habakkuk and Zechariah speak when they say: 'Yahweh is in his holy Temple: let the whole earth be silent before him' (Hab. 2: 20), and 'Let all people be silent before Yahweh, now that he is stirring from his Holy dwelling' (Zech. 2: 17). It is that same awe of which the author of the Revelation to St John the Divine speaks when he writes: 'The Lamb broke the seventh seal, and there was silence in heaven for about half an hour' (Rev. 8: 1). There are times when Christians have been seized by that kind of awe, when silence and adoration are so intertwined that they are totally unaware of anything. They are absorbed in God, yet unable to know that. They are 'caught up right into the third heaven' (2 Cor. 12: 2). People who have described these experiences sometimes say that they did not know where they had been until they returned to themselves: it was only then that they knew that they had been with God, because of the changes that had been wrought in them.

The silence of awe and wonder can teach people when to remain silent, when to withhold even from good speech. Sometimes this is because the experience is indescribable, as it may have been for St Paul when he said:

> this man – still in the body? or outside the body? I do not know, God knows – was caught up into Paradise and heard words said that cannot and may not be spoken by any human being. (2 Cor. 12: 3–4)

Other saints who followed St Paul have described this experience of profound silence and awe in similar ways. There are times also when a revelation from God cannot be spoken: some visionaries have testified to this. One example is that of Lucia Santos who saw the Virgin Mary at Fatima in 1917: she withheld part of her 'secret' from the public for many years.[2]

Paradoxically, silence that is full of awe is closely linked to the kind of speech that Jesus commends to his disciples in times of trial:

> But when you are handed over, do not think about how to speak or what to say; what you are to say will be given to you when the time comes, because it is not you who will be speaking; the Spirit of your Father will be speaking in you. (Matt. 10: 19–20)

By way of contrast, however, there are times of trial when silence has to be total. St Matthew's gospel gives an account of Jesus' silence under questioning. When he was brought before

Pilate, the chief priests and elders Jesus could have replied to the accusations against him. He did not do so, even to save his life (Matt. 27: 14). Since that time some Christian martyrs and confessors have emulated Jesus when they have come to a time of trial. They have not spoken, even to avoid torture or to save their lives.

There are also other occasions when words have to be enfolded into the silence of a person's heart where thought and speech are suspended. Priests and others who hear confessions come to know the intimate details of other people's lives. The words that pass between them have to be received and held in a silence that must last for ever. Those of us who benefit from that kind of silence know it as music that speaks to the depths of our selves and to which we can return with assurance and thankfulness.

Finally, I want to return to the kind of silence which Jeremy found so discordant. He was so afraid of it that he needed to run away from it. This is the silence that reminds us of our own deaths. That kind of silence, 'dead silence', can be positive. It can help us to prepare for death, and the best preparation for death is to live life as well and as fully as possible.

Silences which remind one of death only become truly frightening when we are faced with difficult memories of other people's painful deaths, or when we are afraid of judgement.

The best help we can give ourselves if silence does alarm us, as it did Jeremy, is to seek wise counsel as he did. We need to begin with the Bible, to read and reread the stories of God's mercy (Luke 20: 27–38), to listen to the words that Jesus said on the cross to the penitent thief (Luke 23: 39–43), and that he said to his Father (John 19: 29–30). We need to read the last chapters of all the gospels to hear the good news of the resurrection of Jesus. We can turn eagerly to hear St Paul's great sermons on death (1 Cor. 15) and to see what he says about suffering (Rom. 8: 18–39; 2 Cor. 1: 3–7; Phil. 3: 8–16; Col. 1: 24–9). Since we are human beings we will often need to supplement these strong and comforting passages of scripture with advice and support from other human beings who are wise in respect of our fear of death. Most of us, at some time or another, will need to be reminded that we are born into new life through death, and some of us will need much help from good midwives as we go forward into the great adventure of dying.

It is not morbid to think of death when we are still far away from it. Indeed, I know a nun who is now ninety years old: she has been reflecting on the meaning of death for the past seventy years. She is full of life and interest in the present moment, but that is because she has used long periods of silence to come to terms with death in all its forms.

When people like my nun friend have faced their fears about leave-taking, dying and death, their dead silence can be transformed by God's grace into a warm living silence. I have seen this happen time and again, particularly in convents and among people who live alone. Such people find themselves able to accept the inevitable diminishments, leave-takings and the little deaths of grief, depression and fear with equanimity. They are already alive with resurrection life. They can also help others who are afflicted by fears about the process of dying and judgement after death.

This gift of being able to welcome ultimate silence so as to allow God to transform it into the music of anticipated resurrection life is one that usually comes during one's middle and later years. It may not come at all, for there are still many older people who are afraid of judgement, although they have been taught to rely on God's infinite mercy. There are others who fear extinction, though this fear is voiced far less often today: extinction may feel preferable to the prolongation of life at any cost. Most people seem to come to terms with death by the time they are nearing that moment. While it is still far off, many of us will remain afraid of the process of dying, especially if that is prolonged, or accompanied by much pain, but we come to recognise the naturalness of death itself and its goodness. Silence and aloneness are our chief teachers in these matters, so periods spent alone and in silence can be creative if we allow them to be.

Learning to Use Silence Creatively

If we are to learn to use silence rightly, then we have to attend
to all these aspects of the gift of silence. We cannot learn to be
silent by our own strength, but we can prepare ourselves to
receive God's gifts which we will need if we are to become
people in whom the music of silence can be heard by others.

One of the first things we have to do is to practise the art
of refraining from external noise and internal chatter. We do
this to try to find a restful interior silence in which we can
listen more easily to God. I suspect that most of us find it easier
to practise outward silence when we are alone. We can turn
the radio off and enjoy the warm silence of our own company.
We can go off by ourselves for a long country walk and enjoy
it. We may make ourselves a small prayer corner in a quiet
place in the house and feel at ease there, at any rate for a little
while. We feel comfortable being quiet in our own company
whereas when others are with us we may find their presence
distracting. It is tempting to say something to the other person
that begins a conversation; or they begin one with us and we
feel we must respond out of politeness or love for them.

Internal chatter is harder to manage. Many of us dialogue
with ourselves even when we are alone. Such chatter can be
especially noisy when we find ourselves alone after an exciting
or emotionally disturbing incident or conversation. We need
to stop talking to ourselves if we are to listen to God. I have
already referred to this kind of silence in the earlier chapter on
prayer (see pp. 33ff.), but here I am writing specifically about
the interior silence that is ultimately compatible with activities
of all kinds. One aim is to be able to carry silence with us
wherever we go: another aim is to reach the point where all
our speech can come out of this kind of centred stillness.

Another way of reaching the quiet core of our being is to
stop whatever we are doing for brief periods of time so that
we can disappear into a profound and creative silence in
which we are unaware of anything at all, not ourselves, nor
anything external, nor even God. This kind of silence is very
like sleep, except that when one comes back from this silence
one is instantly alert, aware, alive, energetic in a way that is

different from waking up in the morning and struggling into full consciousness. Nor is it the same as that other kind of absence, which looks like sleep, when, in fact, one is listening attentively to everything that is going on, yet is diving below the surface of what is being said to the meaning and purpose of the words that are being spoken.

The silence of unawareness is well known to those who use transcendental meditation.[3] It is also well known to mystics of every religion. As a Christian I find it important to go into this kind of silence with a clear intention of meeting the three persons of the Trinity. There is, after all, always the danger that one will get hooked on the side effects of this kind of experience and begin to seek the experience rather than God. If that happens, one reaps what one sows, energy that can be misused, that eventually goes sour because it is not being used for God's purposes.

This search for interior silence is a discipline that is not always easy to learn. It is acquired by the practice of stopping one's thoughts for short periods of time. We may need someone else's help if we want to learn to do that. It is worth the temporary humiliation of failure. It is well worth the effort. After a time the deliberate search for moments of silence during each day gives way to a spontaneous ability to go into it at will. At that point we are ready to carry the silence around. It happens quite naturally. It becomes possible to sit in a room full of people talking and be quite at ease and silent until one is approached by someone else. Riding on the top of a bus can be an occasion for quiet. Such silence can coexist happily with external noise and activity. During the 1960s Dag Hammarskjöld, Secretary to the United Nations and one of the busiest men on earth, wrote these words in his personal journal:

> to preserve the silence within – amid all the noise. To remain open and quiet, a moist humus in the fertile darkness where the rain falls and the grain ripens – no matter how many tramp across the parade ground in whirling dust under an arid sky.[4]

Once we have learnt to be silent for short periods it is common to find that these moments coalesce quite easily: silence during times of activity becomes effortless.

It is desirable that our speech should come out of silence, out of attentiveness to what God is saying and doing before one's eyes. It is a good practice when we are beginning to learn about this kind of silence to breathe an arrow prayer to God before, and sometimes during, any conversation. We can ask for the gift of listening carefully to the other person before we attempt to respond. We can ask for time for discernment about what we should say, and whether we should say it at all.

We should, I consider, be quick to think and slow to speak. I have found the discipline advocated by the Sufi masters to be a good one: they say that words should pass through three gates before we speak:

> At the first gate we ask ourselves, 'Are these words true?' If so, we let them pass on; if not, back they go. At the second gate we ask, 'Are they necessary?' At the last gate we ask, 'Are they kind?'[5]

As a Christian I would add a fourth gate: 'Does God want you to say it to this person, now?' If the words can pass through all four gates, one should say them. If not, one should hold them back.

There are things which one knows by the gift of the Holy Spirit about someone else, which one should never say. This is not just a matter of observing confidentiality or confessional secrecy. Those who know how to be quiet inside themselves are often given the gift of discernment into other people's inmost beings, into their hidden thoughts, even at times into their futures.

If we are given that gift of discernment we should always wait upon the Holy Spirit before revealing whatever it is that we 'know' to the person concerned. Our hidden knowledge is given for prayer and for wise waiting. It may create a bond in which the Holy Spirit can give a direct insight to the person with whom we are present. When we see that happening we can be ready to share it. If, however, we pre-empt the Holy Spirit and jump ahead we may do harm. Moreover, if we compound our error by telling people the truth as we see it in an abrupt or harsh way we may inflict great damage on the person to whom we are speaking.

In this matter of discernment we should always remember that we can get wrong messages in prayer and be misled into falsity. So all insights of this kind need to be held in the heart for some time, if not for ever. If, for instance, as once happened to me, you meet a perfectly healthy person, and have a strong intimation that he or she is accompanied by the angel of death, you need to hold that knowledge to yourself, unless there is a very strong leading to speak. You may be wrong. If you are right, it may be too frightening for the person concerned to hear now. If, on the other hand, the person says to you, 'I think there is something seriously wrong with me, though everyone tells me I look very well,' then you have a chance to suggest a visit to the doctor for a check-up instead of replying, as one would be tempted to, 'Don't be so silly!' It's a matter of common sense, but it is surprising how often people blunder because they treat revelations to them as automatically given to them for disclosure to others.

Silence is a great teacher. As Christians we can be the first to extol its benefits and foremost among those who try to show by example how to hear the music of silence that 'beats upon' our 'whorlèd ears' and invites us into the intimacy of God's heart of love.

CHAPTER 9

LOVING GOD'S CREATION

❧

The earth is defiled by the feet of its inhabitants, for they have transgressed the laws, violated the decree, broken the everlasting covenant. (Isa. 24: 4–5)

Love all God's creation, the whole of it and every grain of sand. Love every leaf, every ray of God's light! Love the animals, love the plants, love everything. If you love everything, you will perceive the divine mystery in things. (Dostoyevsky, The Brothers Karamazov)[1]

MEGAN STOOD at the kitchen sink, carefully washing her milk-bottle tops. When they were thoroughly dry, she would put them into a plastic bag to take to her neighbourhood collector.

She turned away and noticed there were a goodly pile of newspapers and washed bottles ready for her to take down to the recycling skips at the refuse dump. There was a pile of cardboard boxes stacked up against the wall. Megan sighed. She would need to pack them flat and tie them up before she could take a carload down to the collection point.

'I haven't got time,' she thought. 'I must get on today. I've got to go to my vegan cooking class this morning, and I'm out this evening. Hywel said he'd take me to a meeting about the excessive use of pesticides in food production.'

She turned the radio on to listen to the early morning farmers' programme. One lead item was about veal production methods. There was another one about the transport of live animals across the English Channel. There was an indignant farmer on the air. He was putting his point of view across: how were he and his colleagues going to live if they didn't sell their surplus male calves for meat production overseas? The proper thing to do was to persuade European farmers to adopt British standards, not to stop exports of live animals. Megan listened sympathetically. That was the kind of thing her father would say.

Megan had grown up on a farm. Her father had a small dairy herd and a goodly flock of sheep for meat production. He was, she knew, a first-class farmer. He reared his animals in good conditions. Recently he had planted a coppice as a conservation exercise, and he and Bronwen grew their own vegetables without using too many artificial fertilisers.

When Megan was fourteen she had decided to become a vegetarian. Dewi hadn't tried to stop her, though he had pointed out that every human being lived on the life of other creatures.

'True,' she retorted, 'but vegetables don't feel in the same way that animals do. You don't have to listen to the cows lowing mournfully when their calves are taken away from them so that we humans can take their mothers' milk.'

She hadn't become a vegan then: it seemed to her to be an excessive gesture, but recently she had decided to look into the whole question of milk production and its links with the disposal of surplus calves: hence her classes in vegan cookery.

Suddenly, Megan felt angry. Being a carer for the environment was hard work, expensive on the family purse, socially embarrassing and awkward for her friends. If she became a vegan she would be even more of a nuisance to friends who might want to invite her to a meal. It was all too much! What good did her small gestures do, anyway? Surely they just amounted to 'a drop in the ocean', a stupid waste of time. Anyway, didn't the Church teach that God gave plants and animals to human beings for them to use as they pleased (Gen. 1: 28–31)? And what would happen to her dad's livelihood if he couldn't sell his surplus male calves? Her thoughts tumbled out over one another so fast that she felt restless, confused and unhappy.

She remembered that it was refuse collection day. With unexpected, sudden and incomprehensible anger, she picked up her milk-bottle tops and bottles, stuffed them into a black plastic bag and took them out to the gate for the collectors. She added the pile of newspapers and threw out all her cardboard boxes. She felt better.

'Later,' she thought, 'I'll tell Hywel I'm not going to be a vegan: it's an absurd kind of protest. But we will go to the meeting about pesticides. I don't like the children taking in all those artificial chemicals with their food.' Then she returned to her housework.

Megan's story illustrates a real dilemma for those who try to do as Dostoyevsky suggests, 'to love all creation'. What does that mean? How do we translate principle into action? If we adopt a particular lifestyle, how can we avoid being judgemental on other people? How can individual actions affect social policy? Those questions must be faced repeatedly by those who decide to adopt alternative lifestyles. First, however, we need to look at the reality of creation as seen in the Bible and our own experience.

Creation's Reality

Christians need not be sentimental about their love of God's creation. The Bible is full of poetry about its beauties, but also full of awe about the destructive forces of nature and of God who is sovereign over nature.[2] One has only to look at the discourses of Yahweh in the book of Job to see creation from the standpoint of the Old Testament writers. Yahweh asks Job: 'Where were you when I laid the earth's foundations? Tell me, since you are so well informed!' (Job 38: 4ff.).

His interrogation is followed by a long series of questions that reduce Job, and all of us, to our true size. Through them we are invited to consider the beauties of nature, for instance, the dawn that God sends:

Have you ever in your life given orders to the morning
or sent the dawn to its post,
 . . . to grasp the earth by its edges
   and shake the wicked out of it?
She turns it as red as a clay seal,
   she tints it as though it were a dress,

stealing the light from evil doers
and breaking the arm raised to strike. (Job 38: 12–15)

In the next verse we are reminded of the power of death:

Have you been right down to the sources of the sea?
and walked about at the bottom of the Abyss?
Have you been shown the gates of Death,
have you seen the janitors of the Shadow dark as death?
(Job 38: 16–17)

At the end of a series of questions, each of them displaying
God's power over the universe, over life and death, Job replies:

My words have been frivolous: what can I reply?
Should I lay my hand over my mouth.
I have spoken once, I shall not speak again;
I have spoken twice, I have nothing more to say. (Job
40: 3–5)

Yahweh goes on relentlessly 'from the heart of the tempest'
(Job 40: 1), to point Job to the magnificence of the animal
kingdom. The description of Behemoth and Leviathan shows
us both the beauty of animals and their power to destroy us
(Job 40: 10—41: 25).

At the end of Yahweh's discourse Job says:

I know that you are all-powerful:
what you conceive, you can perform . . .
Before, I knew you only by hearsay
but now, having seen you with my own eyes,
I retract what I have said,
and repent in dust and ashes. (Job 42: 1; 5–6)

The Old Testament shows us the truth about nature. It is
beautiful. It is also capable of terrible destruction. Many people
know that from experience. In a flood or tempest one seeks
safe sanctuary, or one dies. Earthquakes kill. One does not stop
to admire the magnificence of a lioness when she is on the
prowl to feed her cubs and has a human prey in sight: one
shoots the lioness. It is possible to admire the beauty of a green

mamba as it raises itself to strike, and simultaneously to know that one must kill it, if one wants to survive.[3]

In the New Testament we are given more homely images of nature. Jesus uses the beauty of nature in many of his parables and discourses. He teaches us about the Kingdom of God, for instance in the parable of the sower and the seed (Mark 4: 1–20), the parable of the seed growing by itself (Mark 4: 26–9) and of the mustard seed (Mark 4: 30–2).

Jesus also displays his sovereignity over nature. In St Mark's gospel there is an account of the time when he and his disciples were crossing the sea of Galilee and a storm blew up, terrifying his disciples who were in the boat with him. Jesus 'rebuked the wind . . . and the wind dropped and there was a great calm' (Mark 4: 35–41). Other instances of our Lord's sovereignity over nature are exemplified in the miracle of Cana of Galilee (John 2: 1–12) and the feeding of the hungry beside the sea of Galilee (Mark 6: 30–44).

In his many healing miracles Jesus displays his Godhead through his sovereignity over disease and death. Forty-one distinct instances of physical and mental healing are recorded in the gospels. These include individual and group healings (cf. Mark 6: 53–6). He raised the widow of Nain's son and Lazarus from the grave (Luke 7: 11–17; John 11: 1–43). Although he was done to death, his resurrection shows us the Father's power to raise his Son, and us, to new life, new life that is different from the life we know through the senses of our bodies (1 Cor. 15: 35–53).

The love for all creation that Jesus displays in his teaching, healing miracles and his resurrection helps us, who are his disciples, to see that in his dealings with nature, disease and death God, Father, Son and Spirit, creates a new state of being. God in Jesus takes the offerings of nature, the wind, the water, a loaf of bread and two small fish, the diseased and dead flesh: he transforms them into stillness, wine, abundant food, wholeness, new life. What we are seeing is the glorification of matter through its transformation.

The Divine Mystery of Matter

The quotation from *The Brothers Karamazov* at the head of this chapter comes from a discourse of Father Zossima to his fellow monks. After saying, 'If you love everything, you will perceive the divine mystery in things,' he goes on to say:

> And once you have perceived it, you will begin to comprehend it ceaselessly more and more every day. And you will at last come to love the whole world with an abiding universal love.[4]

It is through love, and only through love, that we who are Christian can perceive the divine mystery, can comprehend it and so come to love it as Christ loves it. This love comes to us through prayer, through listening for the prompting of the Holy Spirit that will show us what God is doing all the time in and through the mysterious changes that are taking place in the material of the universe, the world and all that lives on earth.

As the mystery unfolds, we begin to see that earthquake, flood, forest fire, tempest, suffering, decay and death can coexist and work in harness with the more benign aspects of nature. We come to understand the mysterious transformation that is always taking place as matter is changed by evolution and mutation. It becomes possible to understand the release that decay and death can bring about: we may even see what St Paul saw, namely that:

> what is sown is perishable, but what is raised is imperishable; what is sown is contemptible, but what is raised is glorious; what is sown is a natural body; and what is raised is a spiritual body. (1 Cor. 15: 42–4)

This sowing and raising is going on all the time, both in ourselves and in the whole of creation. Once we see that, we will be careful not to interfere with that process, not to destroy the balance of nature, but to seek to co-operate with God as creation goes through the process of transmutation that will eventually lead to what Teilhard de Chardin called the 'omega point', the point at which the world will become what God wants it to become.

This is no utopian view of the cosmos, nor a figment of imagination, but a reality that is difficult to express. A fourteenth-century mystic and scientist, Nicholas de Cusa, tried to convey its meaning when he said that God is seen beyond the coincidence of contradictories. In a passage that is elegant, yet somewhat difficult for our modern minds to grasp, he writes:

> Howbeit, this coincidence is a contradiction without contradiction, even as an end without an end . . . And Thou, Lord, sayest unto me that, just as otherness in unity is without otherness because it is unity, even so, in infinity, contradiction is without contradiction, because it is infinity . . . Therein the opposition of opposites is an opposition without opposition, just as the end of things finite is an end without an end.[5]

Centuries later the scientist and priest Teilhard de Chardin found himself alone in the steppes of Asia on the Feast of the Transfiguration in 1923. Being alone, and without bread and wine, he was unable to celebrate a Eucharist. Instead he meditated on the eucharistic presence of Christ through the universe. He wrote a passionate prayer to God that expressed some of his ideas about apparent contradictions in nature:

> The consecration of the world would have remained incomplete, a moment ago, had you not with special love vitalized for those who believe, not only life-bringing forces, but also those that bring death. My communion would be incomplete – would quite simply, not be Christian – if, together with the gains which this new day brings me, I did not also accept, in my own name and in the name of the world, as the most immediate sharing in your own being, those processes, hidden or manifest, of enfeeblement, of ageing, of death which increasingly consume the universe, to its salvation or its condemnation.[6]

It could be held that all that we see happening in creation, the apparent opposites of suffering and glory, is 'contradiction without contradiction' within eternity. We do not need to posit God as the author of all our sufferings to realise that God is at work within nature's suffering and death. That realisation, however, should not turn us into quietists, puppets who are indifferent to anything that is happening because of human action in the world, people who think that the world is doomed to extinction and that the quicker it happens, the better.

Scientists tell us that the world is finite, that it will end. Christians agree with that view: they believe in the second coming of Christ; they also believe that matter, created by God, is sacred. It must, therefore, be cherished rather than be destroyed by human negligence, indifference and greed. When God chooses to end it is God's affair, not ours. We should do nothing on this earth that will destroy it. On the contrary, human beings, created in God's image, can help nature in its evolution. They can use its products, and even improve on them, but they do need to think long and hard before they do anything that interferes with the balance of nature and disturbs the relationships within creation, especially as everything is related to everything else.

A twentieth-century professor and priest, John Polkinghorne, sees the connectedness of everything. He writes:

> Reality is a multi-layered unity. I can perceive another person as an aggregation of atoms, an open biochemical system in interaction with the environment, a specimen of homo sapiens, an object of beauty, someone whose needs deserve my respect and compassion, a brother for whom Christ died. All are true and all mysteriously coin-here in that one person. To deny one of these levels is to diminish both that person and myself, the perceiver; to do less than justice to the richness of reality. Part of the case for theism is that in God the Creator, the ground of all that is, these different levels find their lodging and their guarantee. He is the source of connection, the one whose creative act holds in one the world-views of science, aesthetics, ethics and religion as expressions of his reason, joy, will and presence.[7]

These authors have been quoted at some length because I think that those who are called to 'love all God's creation' need to see nature in her fullness. Our intercession and witness should come from a theological perspective rather than from some romantic consideration of the beauties of nature and/or a sentimental feeling for plants and animals.

Prayer and Witness

When we set out to 'love everything' we will soon find out how difficult that is to do, because we human beings have an innate tendency to put our own interests first. Those often conflict with what our consciences suggest we should be doing. If, for instance, we decide to boycott a particular product because the manufacturers have designed something that interferes with the ozone layer above the earth's atmosphere, we may find that the products we buy instead are not nearly so good as the ones produced by the errant manufacturer. Conscience pulls one way, desire for an effective product the other!

When we act unselfishly, as Megan did in the story that heads this chapter, we are likely to find out how difficult it is to persevere with our good actions. It is, for example, time-consuming and often expensive to buy recycled products, take our rubbish for recycling, look for organically grown vegetables, avoid products whose testing involves cruelty to animals, change our eating habits to conform to the demands of our consciences. Small wonder, then, that so many of us give up almost as soon as we have begun!

Whenever we consider matters that relate to our environment, we should listen carefully to both sides of any questions about collective policy before we pray and decide what action to take. Environmental issues are contentious. Our collective decisions can destroy nature's balance. They can affect the financial welfare of human beings in industries that use the natural products of the environment like coal, wood, plants and animals. They can affect the ozone layer, vegetation and animal population of our planet. Individual and collective decisions and actions can affect the quantity and quality of human life on earth.

Sometimes it is easy to see how any collective policy can be harmful, or beneficial, to environment and human beings alike. Any governmental policy, for instance, which permits unrestricted fishing in waters that are already denuded of their natural fish through excessive consumption is bound to be harmful to the environment and fishermen alike, to say nothing of the rest of us who no longer can enjoy fish as a food. On the other hand, our instinctive delight in the beauty of whales and seals may have to give way to the necessity of culling them if the balance of nature is to be kept and the fish population is to be maintained.

There are no easy solutions, no obvious Christian attitudes towards these kinds of issue. What is, I believe, important is that none of us dodge them on the grounds of ignorance, indifference or inability to do anything directly about them. These are important questions to humanity.

God certainly acts through all kinds of people, including those who have no religious faith, but for those of us who are Christians, prayer is an important way of asking for God's guidance. The Holy Spirit will give us the insights we need, but it seems that in this, as in so many other issues, at first only a relatively few of us respond with creative and practical action. There does come a time, however, when the insights gain ground, the pace changes. Eventually, the issues become so important to so many people that they become collectively willing to bring pressure to bear on governments, non-governmental agencies and multinational corporations. That is when a true change in world policy can take place.

In the long term this is true, but in the short term we may find ourselves at any point in this process. At any given moment, we may see our own efforts in prayer and action to be puny and unfruitful. We may not live long enough to see the harvest of our prayer in our own lifetimes, but that does not matter. We are part of a movement towards the 'omega point' when all creation will find its fulfilment through Christ. That movement is taking place all over the world, and it is not confined to Christians.

One of the most moving appeals to Western civilisations that has ever been made has come from the Kogi people who live in the Sierra Nevada de Santa Maria, near the northern limit of the Andes in Colombia, South America. This small and disappearing tribe, descendants of an ancient Tairona civilisation, was visited by a BBC producer, Alan Ereira, and a film team. The Kogi asked this film crew to convey to the Western world their anxieties about the way in which human beings were despoiling God's creation. Their own civilisation being older, they call us 'the Younger Brother' in the message which Ereira relayed through his film and a subsequent book. In one part of it they say:

> Up to now we have ignored the Younger Brother. We have not even deigned to give him a slap . . . But now we can no longer look after the world alone. The Younger Brother is doing too much damage. He must see and understand and assume responsibility. Now we will have to work together. Otherwise the world will die.[8]

We need to heed their message. We also need to offer the energy of our love to Christ that he might use it on behalf of creation. If we do that the Holy Spirit may prompt us to some practical action.

Practical Ways of Showing Our Love for God's Creation

We should never laugh at the Megans of this world. Their individual efforts to collect tinfoil, recycle paper and bottles and take other actions to save our environment are immensely important when put together with other people's efforts. We may not be able to be as caring as they are, but many of us can find ways of being good personal stewards of our small piece of creation, our material goods, our gardens, our foodstuffs. We have to do it in our own way, but if we do not do something we shall impoverish our world and its atmosphere.

The care of our environment is an area where Christians and non-Christians can readily join with each other to prophesy and work for better ways of being stewards of creation. The Green movement is well known. 'Life Style', started some thirty years ago by the Very Reverend Horace Dammers, is its Christian equivalent, though less well known.[9] The Third World Movement, World Development Movement, Plant-a-Tree for Posterity Movement, the World Wildlife Fund and many other organisations have broadly based policies on the conservation of the world's environment, the elimination of pollution and the conservation of nature. To these must be added organisations that care for the welfare of domesticated animals, such as the Royal Society for the Prevention of Cruelty to Animals and Compassion in Farming, and organisations that seek to help human beings, such as the National Society for the Prevention of Cruelty to Children, Amnesty International, Christian Aid, OXFAM, Catholic Action for Overseas Development (CAFOD) and Traidcraft.

Christians, thank God, can be found in all these environmental and animal welfare organisations, and also in human relief agencies. As a Christian individual I find myself able to support some of these organisations but, for me personally, symbolic action has been an important way of reminding myself of environmental issues: it earths my prayer.

In describing some of the symbolic and practical actions that are important for me, I am only giving examples in order to indicate the links between prayer, symbol, and action. Each person has to find his or her own linkages. For instance, the wooden cross that I wear was carved for me out of rain forest wood. When I bought it from the artist who designed and made it, he sent the money to the Tairona Trust to help the Kogi people. Whenever I take that cross in my hands, I am reminded of the Kogi people's message to the world. I am reminded of environmental issues. I am prompted to prayer.

When I go shopping, I buy recycled products. I also buy certain consumable goods from firms that pay their Third World producers proper prices. These actions help me to pray and work for justice and peace in our world.

I became a vegetarian about twenty years ago at a time when I realised how many bushels of grain were needed to produce a large juicy steak for me to enjoy. That grain could feed many starving people in some Third World countries, if we in the northern hemisphere ate less meat. Later, I used my vegetarianism to remind me to work for better conditions for animals that are used for food production. Since I myself kill vegetables in order to stay alive, I have no objection in principle to killing animals, as long as it is done humanely: when I was younger I cooked meat and fish for my family. Nevertheless, I abhor the cruelty that is involved in some food production processes. I therefore support efforts to curb any forms of production methods that involve deliberate cruelty to animals and human beings.

Trying to do all this without seeming 'holier than thou' to my relatives, colleagues and friends has been, and is, no easy task. At times, I have been thankful that I now live alone, and generally eat alone. Although I feel I cannot be true to my own calling to prayer without finding a symbolic and practical expression of the insights that come to me through prayer, I am genuinely happy that other Christians take a different point of view. Very few of my friends, for instance, are vegetarian. Relatively few buy recycled products. Some buy things from manufacturers who have bad marketing records in Third World countries. Others have no trouble buying eggs from battery hens. They remain my good friends. I remain theirs.

What the Holy Spirit says or does not say to other people is not my responsibility, but it is my task to urge all Christians to consider the issues concerning God's creation carefully, to pray about them and to take whatever action seems to them to be appropriate. For in the end, I believe, it will be the 'coincidence of contradictories', our joint endeavours, which will help God to bring creation to its fulfilment.

CHAPTER 10

MAKING PEACE

෯෧

Peace I bequeath to you, my own peace I give
you, a peace which the world cannot give, this
is my gift to you. (John 14: 27)

Live in peace yourself and then you can bring
peace to others. (Thomas à Kempis, *The Imitation
of Christ*)[1]

'PUT YOUR body on the line!' Matthew looked up, startled.
His friend Nicky stood behind him.

'What did you say?'

'I said: put your body on the line. You're always talking
about peace. OK. Show me you mean it. There's a march from
Aldermaston to London next week, after term has broken up.
Come with me.'

'I can't, I've got to work in the "vac"; I've got finals in June.
You're all right: your finals are still two years away.'

'I may not be alive to do them. You don't understand,
Matthew. This is urgent. If we don't stop this proliferation of
nuclear weapons, our children will never be born.'

'You always exaggerate. Anyway, didn't you hear that speech
the other day, the one that made a very good case for our
keeping the "bomb" as a deterrent?'

'Yes, I heard it. Rubbish, I thought. If you have a deterrent, you have to be prepared to use it. Look at Hiroshima and
Nagasaki. What we've got now are far more terrible than the
atom bomb. We'd let ours fly. The other side would know.
They'd just have time to let theirs fly at us before they were
blown to bits, and so were we. It's all a dreadful waste of money:

we could feed millions of hungry people in the world if we didn't spend so much money on arms.'

'It's not as simple as that. Anyway, I'm not coming.'

It is now thirty-five years since I overheard that conversation, which was typical of many that I heard in the 1960s. During those years and the subsequent two decades the possibility of nuclear warfare preoccupied many people in our Western world. The dread of a nuclear holocaust was so great that people of my generation thought about it more than any other single political issue. Many of us tried to stop the proliferation of nuclear weapons. We were quite angry about our contemporaries who would not take action.

At the time of the conversation I had small children, so my concern was for them and for their children. Since then there have been some changes in the way warfare is conducted. The major powers in the world are now beginning to work together to scale down their caches of nuclear weapons. Peace has come to some places in the world that were formerly at war. We are not, however, out of the wood: territorialism is prevalent all over the world.

Territorialism and Violence

Human beings are territorial animals. Their desire for territory is innate. They have tried to exert some control over their warring propensities by establishing the United Nations. It is the best international peace-keeping body that we have; yet it remains difficult to secure and maintain peace in a world where different tribes and peoples claim particular territory.

Although the threat of satellite warfare and intercontinental nuclear war may have diminished a little, conventional warfare has become more sophisticated and dreadful. Aggressors, and sometimes those who rise against them, stop at nothing. They condone genocide. They consent to the wholesale destruction of civilians. They sometimes use chemical and germ warfare. They encourage terrorism. They indulge in torture and the degradation of human beings. They permit rape and pillage.

They hijack innocent people, imprison and sometimes kill them to gain publicity for their points of view.

Since the arrival of satellite communication and widespread television and radio coverage of world news, it has been impossible to hide what is happening. Whole populations of people have been alerted to the atrocities that can be committed by human beings against each other when they are fighting over territory. The horrors of Auschwitz and its companion death camps now serve only to remind us of the terrible atrocities that are still being committed in our world today.

Participants in wars cannot be expected to stop fighting for what they believe to be right unless the negotiations for peace bring them justice. They can, however, long for peace, pray for peace, welcome peace when it also brings justice.

Those of us who are spectators of other people's wars throughout the world generally abhor what we see happening before our eyes. Even when we feel that a particular war is justified, many of us, perhaps most of us, are becoming aware of a great desire in the world to find better ways of solving territorial and other international disputes than by going to war. However, before we look at what individuals can do to foster peace in countries other than their own, we need to pay careful attention to violent behaviour within our own societies and communities.

Violence in Individuals

Each human being contains within himself or herself the whole world. Each person has the potential to become a violent aggressor or a victim of aggression. Each contains the seeds of anger that, if let loose, can erupt into overt violent behaviour. We may not like to admit that fact, but we need to do so if we are to understand the role of Christians in peacemaking.

We behave aggressively because we are human beings: however, we also learn about aggression as a manipulative form of behaviour from an early age because it often seems to be the only way by which our needs can be satisfied. Whenever our various angers and frustrations cannot be satisfied, or channelled in appropriate ways, they may erupt into outward aggression.

Most parents know that very well and spend a lot of their children's formative years helping them to gain control of their aggressive emotions so that they can use anger creatively. One of the most important lessons we have to learn as children and young adults is that the energy of anger is not bad in itself. We can be angry in right ways. Jesus himself exhibited righteous anger from time to time (Matt. 23; Luke 19: 45–8). As we shall see later in this chapter, anger can be used creatively in many ways, including social and political reform, creative art, peace-making, humanitarian aid and intercession. Nevertheless few of us use anger creatively all the time. Most of us can admit that we often use it destructively.

As individuals we often experience conflict within ourselves. We feel frustrated and need to let out our pent-up feelings about, for instance, being unhappy at home, unemployed, poor, underprivileged, rejected, oppressed. We may feel anxious and insecure and use aggression as a form of self-defence. We may unconsciously despise a feature of our own characters, see it in others, and vent our anger on them instead of on ourselves. Some of us are quite unaware of our anger: other people will recognise its presence through our non-verbal behaviour and tone of voice. Some of us who are accused in this way may have bottled up our anger without realising it: it lurks below the surface of our consciousness and may erupt without warning at any time. We will do well to heed our accusers and try to find the cause of our unacceptable behaviour: however, we are not always to blame; other people can project their own anger on to us and then act towards us as if we were angry with them! Anger that has its roots in frustration, fear, self-loathing and hatred can lead to violence.

Most of us meet violence for the first time inside our own homes. Ever since human beings began to live together members of the same family have displayed aggressive behaviour towards each other on occasion. Physical, mental and verbal cruelty are commonplace between spouses, live-in partners, parents and children. Marital rape exists. Granny-bashing, spouse-beating and child abuse occur in all social classes.

There is now some evidence that there are links between domestic violence and social violence outside the home. There may be a direct correlation between seeing violent films and videos and antisocial behaviour outside the home. Certainly violence outside the home appears to be on the increase and a worrying feature is that quite young children are now committing violent crimes. I have had personal contact with two young children who killed a baby. In the last two years most people who watch the news on television must have been saddened by the killing of a toddler by two lads,[2] and the murder of an old lady on her way to church by a fourteen-year-old youth.[3]

Moreover, anger can be whipped up when angry people get together in pairs, small groups, gangs and tribes. Organised robbery with violence is common on the streets of our big cities. Gang rape is an act of aggression rather than a sexual act. Footballers fight each other and their fans on the pitch. Fans erupt in frustrated anger when their heroes let them down. Riots occur. Violence breaks out between police and protesters at marches and demonstrations that were intended to be peaceful. Tribal warfare is a way of life for many underprivileged young people living in deprived circumstances. All these demonstrations of communal violence come into the front rooms of our houses through news programmes, documentaries and fictionalised accounts of real events.

Anger, righteous and unrighteous, is a feature of human existence. In the past fifty years we have seen too much of destructive anger, too close to hand, both through personal experience of war and through the media. In consequence, many of us have become desensitised to what is going on in us and in all around us. It is not surprising that some of us, who do recognise the extent of the problems arising out of human aggression, are tempted to avoid getting entangled in any action that might bring violence into our own lives. We may still be wanting to avoid looking at our own anger or its physical effects on us and other people. Those of us who are Christians, however, really have no option.

God has given us as Christians the ministry of reconciliation. He has 'entrusted to us the message of reconciliation', and he has called us to be 'ambassadors for Christ' (cf. 2 Cor. 5: 18–20). In order to fit ourselves for that work we need to face the size and extent of our own pugnacity before embarking on any attempt at peacemaking.

In my personal experience the Bible has been the greatest help in allowing me to admit to my own capacity for aggression and violence. The Bible is full of stories about war, blood-curdling aggression, murder, rape, theft, suppression of human rights and dignities. When I was a child, I read these stories eagerly: they often told me about how God would use righteous anger to bring destruction on evil people, for example the Egyptians who persecuted my heroes, the Israelites (Exod. 5–14). They told me how people like Jael and Judith could be God's agents through violence (Judg. 4: 12–22; Judith 8–16). Stories about Abraham and Moses told me it was all right to want other people's territory (Gen. 12ff.; Num. 33–4). It was a relief to listen to the anger in some psalms (e.g. Ps. 58; 68: 21–3; 137: 7–9). I was not unduly dismayed by the New Testament either, because Jesus showed anger and impatience at times, as when he overturned the tables of the money-changers in the temple (John 2: 13–17; Luke 19: 45–6), and when he castigated the Pharisees (Matt. 23: 1–39). Some of what St Paul did and said seemed to me to originate from his impatience and anger with some of the people he wrote to, and about, in his letters to the young Churches. The Bible validated my own feelings, made me feel that they were shared by other religious people and made me less afraid of their strength in my life.

It was when I grew up, however, and came across Jesus' teaching about forgiveness and love for one's enemy that I began to struggle with internal conflicts over my aggressive tendencies that were really difficult to live with. The whole of the Sermon on the Mount descended on me almost as soon as I became a practising Christian when I was eighteen years old. All of it was a challenge to my discipleship, but certain verses stood out. These sentences impaled themselves on my mind and heart and refused to go away: 'Love your enemy and pray for those who persecute you' (Matt. 5: 44); 'You must therefore set no bounds to your love, just as your heavenly Father sets none to his' (Matt. 5: 48). The words 'Do not judge, and you will not be judged; do not condemn, and you will not be condemned; forgive, and you will be forgiven' (Luke 6: 36–7) burnt themselves into my consciousness. Jesus' reply to Peter when the latter asked him about how often he was to forgive his enemies struck me as uncompromising, and impossible for ordinary mortals to do (Matt. 18: 21–2).

I struggled because at that time I did not like my own anger. I could not see how it could be used in the service of God. I thought that you could only achieve peace by surrender to the aggressor. I wanted to forgive, but found it hard to do so. I was frightened by the strength of my feelings over certain peace and justice issues, such as racism, sexism and militarism. I had to learn how God takes violence and uses it as a means to reconciliation. I had to give my anger to Jesus, the Christ.

God's Way with Violence

In our redemption story we find that God uses our sin, anger and aggression to bring about our salvation through Christ's atoning death. When I was younger I struggled for a long time before I could accept the necessity of the atonement, that act of violence by which our redemption was effected. It meant learning to be humble enough to accept that I was 'bought with a price' (1 Cor. 6: 20; 7: 23), that God appointed Christ 'as a sacrifice for reconciliation, through faith, by the shedding of his blood' (Rom. 3: 25) and that through that act God 'justifies everyone who has faith in Jesus' (Rom. 3: 26). The words are difficult, the concepts behind them more so, and their re-enactment in the central act of the Eucharist even more difficult again. Indeed, like many other people I rebelled against what seemed to be a cannibalistic rite of Holy Communion.

Later, I came to understand it better, partly through reading the works of René Girard and his commentators,[4] partly through seeing sacrificial love in action in my own home, partly through going beyond feeling to participation in the Eucharist. My feelings now are summed up for me by some words that I read recently in Paul Tournier's *The Violence Inside*:

> The Christian religion still has its supreme rite in the Eucharist, a symbolic manifestation of violence, commem-

orating and renewing the Sacrifice of Christ, and ensuring
the mystic communion of the faithful who together eat
his body and drink his blood.[5]

Later, Tournier comments about what this sacrifice does for us:

> In the case of sacrifice, however, it is as if all men found
> themselves united as they direct and discharge this poten-
> tial of violence from their hearts upon a single object, the
> victim of a solemn sacrifice, which cannot take its revenge.
> Now at last the community is saved, and that is why René
> Girard calls this violence 'inaugural', because it inaugurates
> society. Sacrifice restores the harmony of the community.[6]

It took a long time for me to accept that I needed to project
my violence on to Christ. It took even longer to understand
how vital it was to do this in the prayer of intercession for
reconciliation.

The greatest gift of those years of wrestling with theories
about the atonement has been the realisation that this work of
peacemaking, or reconciliation, has been accomplished by
Christ through his work on the cross (Eph. 2: 11–22). It was
done 'once for all' (Rom. 6: 10), yet because it was done
eternally, Christ's self-offering is still effective in time. Christians
are called to be God's temples (1 Cor. 3: 16). They will be
aware of Christ's dying and rising in themselves and others.
Christ suffers when we suffer, Christ dies when we die, and
because Christ, the sinless one, was raised from the dead, so
we, God's adopted sons and daughters, are raised with him.
Christians are happy, as St Paul was, to experience in their own
bodies 'the hardships that still have to be undergone by Christ
for the sake of his body, the Church' (Col. 1: 24). This is the
work to which we are all called in and through prayer and
peaceable action. Some of us will be called to more specific
ways of praying and working for peace: our journey may be a
hard one.

Praying and Peacemaking

The first task for anyone who takes peacemaking through prayer seriously is to make peace within himself or herself. This can be a difficult task to undertake. It would be absurd to refrain from praying for peace for others until one was at perfect peace with oneself. One would never begin! We have to combine our search for inner peace with a sincere desire to pray for true reconciliation in many different situations. I, for instance, have spent many years of my life learning how to forgive, how to channel my anger creatively, how to learn to allow Christ to reconcile the warring elements in my own personality that hinder me from being able to bring peace to others. During those long years I have struggled and needed the help of wiser and older people than I, but I have also been able to pray with and for other people who are searching for true peace.

Peace within ourselves can only come if we are truly at peace with God, so it can only be accomplished by the grace of God. Our co-operation with God involves recognising that our own faults are probably greater than those of other people. It means being quick to repent after sin. We should turn to God so often that we are always penitent, always asking to be changed into God's likeness. We have to be prompt to forgive those who injure us, especially when we need to forgive ourselves. It means incorporating our own violence into our personalities and using our anger creatively. I do not believe this work can be done by purely psychological means. It is dependent on a recognition that there is an essential unity between good and evil, disruption and harmony, violence and gentleness, dark and light. Undoubtedly some non-Christians are able to integrate their negative qualities into their personalities in such a way that they become whole persons. Christians, however, recognise that it is Christ who takes our violence and transforms it into peace by his sacrifice on the cross. They never take the credit for their own wholeness, but always give the glory to God.

To do this kind of internal peacemaking we will need a certain detachment from our own turbulent feelings. We need to dwell in the peace of Christ, in his reconciling heart. Once we have known the kind of peace that comes from a thankful recognition of our own salvation, we feel so secure in God's love that we cannot easily forget it. Then we begin to radiate God's love and peace and joy to other people. This is not an impossible goal, for with God all things are possible, and God undoubtedly does enable some people to grow into that kind of peace during their lifetime. There is a moving description of what can happen in Iulia de Beausobre's fictionalised account of the life of St Seraphim, an eighteenth-century Russian Orthodox monk.[7]

For many years Seraphim lived alone in a hut deep in the heart of a Russian forest near his monastery at Sarov. There he prayed and strove for inner peace. There he learnt to forgive. Through days and nights of vigil he learnt the meaning of love through silence, suffering and combat with unseen forces of evil. Iulia de Beausobre tells us:

> Slowly, very slowly, the enclosing darkness was overcome. Out of the place called Serafim, the light of the spirit shone into the enclosing body of blasphemy, causing it to loosen its grip, waver, fall away, dissolve. It took a thousand days and a thousand nights to achieve it.[8]

Eventually, after a period of even greater seclusion, Seraphim came to 'the muted joy of perfect peace'.[9] Some time later he left his solitary way of life and became available to others. His door was frequently unlocked. Those who came found their peace simply by being near him. One man, Nicholas Motovilov, whom Seraphim had healed, looked into his eyes and found himself enveloped in a radiance that obliterated Seraphim's features. He was overcome by a sense of loveliness, sweetness, quiet peace, joy, warmth, heavenly scent. Seraphim told him:

> 'The grace of God is in you and you are in it. If you could only see how your face shines. Will you always remember the grace that has been lavished on you, my joy?'
> 'And me not even a monk!'
> 'That's nothing. It is to the man, not to his state or

condition, that God says, "Child give me your heart." If we give it, he comes.'[10]

I have quoted from this account of St Seraphim's life at length because, although few people live eremitical lives, many people do undertake this task of giving their hearts to God with the desire to become people of peace, and a considerable number succeed. Many of us can be like Nicholas. We can catch peace from other people who are peaceful themselves: indeed, I have myself had this experience of being with people who radiate joy and peace: I have benefited even from short times in their presence. They remind me that Thomas à Kempis said: 'Live in peace yourself, and then you can bring peace to others.'[11] Seraphim of Sarov said: 'Find peace in yourself, and a thousand around you will find their peace.'[12] Yes, the witness of a peaceful and peaceable person is a glorious way of giving glory to God and creating a climate where others can find their own peace.

In our ministry of intercession and reconciliation there are two kinds of prayer for peace, general prayer and specific prayer. Christians all over the world, whether they be pacifists or supporters of just wars, are joining people of other faiths to pray for world peace every day at noon. They recite a simple prayer composed by Satish Kumar. It goes like this:

Lead me from darkness to light,
Lead me from falsehood to truth,
Lead me from war to peace.
Let peace fill our minds, our hearts,
our world, our universe.[13]

They pray with zeal and perseverance. They watch the news and pray for reconciliation between individuals and groups who are in dispute with each other. They pray for those families where there is marital disharmony. They pray ahead of, during and after events that are likely to be contentious. Week after week individuals, groups and Church congregations pray for peace in this general way. Their contribution to peacemaking is considerable, for through prayer they are creating a climate of love in which negotiation, peaceful solutions and reconciliation can take place.

Sometimes Christians will find themselves called to a more specific role in peacemaking. This may happen at a personal level, or it may happen through contact with a situation at a distance through media knowledge and/or prayer. People who are called to this kind of prayer are often pulled into it by duty, close relationship or compassion. To illustrate what I mean it is easier to begin with a concrete example taken from my own professional life.

As a professional person when I listen to an unhappily married couple I will also be praying for them, ahead of the interview, at the time and afterwards. In a mysterious way the people concerned are incorporated into my own inner life. They are literally 'brought to Jesus' and held there in love while he works to reconcile them. I pray with confidence, knowing that the Lord Jesus will win the victory. That does not always mean that the two people, or two groups, 'will live happily ever after'. Often they do not.

Sometimes the couple cannot hear God's invitation to forgive, to make peace: they continue to be at war with each other. If that happens there is little that I can do, except to go on praying. It may, however, be right to stop being a sponge for their mutual hostility. In that case I stop praying in this intimate though hidden way and simply go on praying for them in a more general way.

There are occasions when Christ enables two people, or groups of people, to stop hurting each other by inviting them to separate. This is not failure: it is victory of a particular kind. In time the wounds they have inflicted on each other may heal. In time they may come to see that separation has enabled each to grow and develop in ways that would have been impossible had they stayed together. They may even become thankful for their time together and grateful to God for what has taken place since they went on their separate ways.

At other times, healing is delayed. God may show all those who are involved that they are trying for good results too quickly. They may need some breathing space, a change of direction, a change of counsellor. They may need a different kind of help. Every counsellor should ask God for the grace of discernment to know when to stop, when to advise a couple or a group to find alternative help. It can be a greater help to withdraw than to press on because one is afraid of failing the people who have entrusted themselves to one's care.

There are times, happily, when all involved are rewarded by true reconciliation. When it happens, it is always accompanied by signs of new life. Just as Christ's death is succeeded by resurrection life, so the visible death of a wrong element in a relationship, or even of the relationship itself, can be followed by a new relationship based upon transformed attitudes.

It is, I have found, very difficult to predict when this is likely to happen. One sign that gives me hope is when both sides are willing to listen to each other's point of view. Another comes when they are ready to meet across the divide, however huge it is. Hope increases whenever there is a mutual agreement to look for ways through apparent impasses. Lastly, it burgeons when forgiveness is in the air. As all negotiators, mediators, counsellors and therapists know, miracles do occur: so do disasters and the dividing line between the two is very thin. Often success comes when each side feels understood by the other, when they are using language in the same way, when they can allow the past to be forgiven, and when each knows that a reconciliation will be mutually beneficial.

I have used a couple in marital disharmony as an illustration but what I have said applies equally to the kind of work some of us are called to in mediating between groups of people who are in dispute. It also applies to an even more hidden ministry of prayer that comes through a direct and specific call from God to pray for people whom one does not know at all in one's ordinary life and yet does know through Christ.

Those who undertake such hidden prayer are usually called into it through a sense of identification with the people who ask for, or need, our prayers. We are moved by compassion for them. We need to be firmly attached to God and equally attached, but in a dispassionate way, to the people with and for whom we are praying. We are, as it were, providing the meeting place in our heart. It is clear that it is Christ who is doing the work of reconciliation; yet, since we are 'in Christ' through baptism we share in his work in a real way. The work may be done quietly, almost without the intercessor being aware of it, but there are times when the full strength of the conflict between the warring individuals may be experienced in one's own self. Sometimes it feels as if one is part of the battle as well as being a battlefield.[14] Since the price of Christ's work was, and is, grievous, its cost may be reflected in the invisible scars of battle which are inflicted on the person of the intercessor.

This kind of specific yet hidden intercession is taxing on energy and strength. Those who pray in this way owe it to God to take care of themselves. At times, one needs more rest. At times, one needs to be able to hide away while the conflict rages. In this sanctuary of withdrawal one has to wait in a kind of thick fog, a miasma of hatred, bitterness, even despair, for Christ's rescue. The waiting may at times seem intolerable. Yet, in God's own time and way, the fog does lift. If one is called to this ministry then God's grace is abundant. Usually the withdrawal can be an interior one and no one else is aware of it at all. If physical retreat into seclusion becomes necessary God gives one the strength to carry on one's outward life until a temporary withdrawal becomes possible. The retreat into solitude can be interrupted by official duty or a call of charity without loss of focus. In a mysterious way God hides this work from anyone who does not understand it, but will sometimes send a beleaguered servant a friend in time of need. Truly, God is good to those whom he calls to this kind of ministry.

It is vital that those who pray, and those whose prayer shapes their counsel, never lose hope. 'For God everything is possible' (Matt. 19: 26); we have to believe that by faith, and if the outcome seems disastrous to us, we must continue to believe that God will use even tragedy to bring about a good outcome that we cannot yet discern. I want to illustrate this by telling one final story about a would-be peacemaker who was a failure.

On 13 October 1536, Robert Aske, Yorkshireman by birth, attorney and fellow of Gray's Inn, accepted an invitation to lead a 'Pilgrimage of Grace' to petition King Henry VIII to rescind Thomas Cromwell's policy of suppressing the monasteries and convents throughout the land, a policy which had begun in earnest that year. By the end of the year Aske had assembled between thirty and forty thousand men from Lincolnshire, Yorkshire and the northern counties. Those in power were alarmed; indeed, the Archbishop of York took refuge in Pontefract Castle. The Duke of Norfolk and the Earl of Shrewsbury were sent to quell the angered pilgrims. So strong was Aske's character, so clear his vision, that he was able to negotiate with them. They gave him safe conduct so that he could put his case to Henry VIII. He did so eloquently, and thought he had won Henry over. When he returned north early in 1537, he judged that the pilgrims' grievances had been redressed. He believed that the religious houses would be left in peace. He thought that together they had discerned God's mind. He thought that he had secured justice and peace.

Instead, he was to find that neither side really wanted peace. A fresh outbreak of rebellion from some of the less trusting pilgrims gave Thomas Cromwell, Vicar General, and Henry's advisers the excuse they needed to quell the Pilgrimage of Grace. They broke their word to Aske, seized him, tried him for treason and sentenced him to a cruel death at York where, in July 1537, he was hanged in chains.

There is no doubt that Aske thought he was right, that he had been given a vision of what God wanted to happen to the monasteries and convents of the land. He also thought of himself as a peaceable man. True, he had amassed enough supporters for a show of strength, but his intentions were to win his cause through peaceful negotiations. He found out, as so many before and since have found out, that anyone who tries to be a peacemaker may have to drink the bitter cup of failure.

Some four hundred years later a remarkable novel about Aske was published by Hilda M. Prestcott.[15] It is called *A Man on a Donkey*. In it there is a passage about Aske's cruel death.

And as his eye told him of the sickening depth beneath his body, and as mind foreknew the lagging endlessness of torment below him, so, as if the lightening had brought an inner illumination also, he knew the greater gulf of despair above which his spirit hung helpless and aghast.

God did not now nor would in any furthest future, prevail. Once He had come, and died. If He ever came again, again He would die, and again, and so for ever, by His own will rendered powerless against the free and evil wills of men.

Then Aske met the full assault of darkness without reprieve of hoped for light, for God ultimately vanquished was no God at all. But yet, though God was not God, as the head of the dumb worm turns, so his spirit turned, blindly, gropingly, helplessly loyal, towards that good, that holy, that merciful, which though not God, was still the last dear love of a vanquished and tortured man.[16]

An old wise woman, Malle, witnesses this death, sees in it the profound identification between Aske and Christ and says to a young companion of hers words that sum up for me Christ's work of reconciliation on the cross:

'So is He gone down under those waves.' She lifted her head and her eyes widened. 'Look!' she said. 'The Dale's full of light. He has set on fire the sea. Not even the deep waters can quench Him, but He comes again, flaming and shining, with the bitter sea itself to be His new coat. Hurt and harm are His coat, and a glory that the young stars didn't know. Light has licked up the dark water. Love has drunk sorrow, rejoicing, and the great Angel of Pain is redeemed.'[17]

Aske's life and Prestcott's book speak to me about reconciliation in ways that pass my understanding yet speak to the depths of my being. It seems to me that this 'failure' represents a victory that only those who follow Christ to the cross and who are content to be crucified with him (Gal. 2: 20) can know about. For to be the battle as well as the battlefield, as Aske was, is also by faith to be part of the gift of Easter. In this prayer of blind faith, of turning 'as the head of a dumb worm turns', we are, unknown to ourselves, the means by which our Lord Jesus Christ triumphs over evil.

Peacemakers like Aske exist in all generations. Their particular call always involves the gift of themselves to God to be used in whatever way God chooses. Their vocations have to be lived out in various ways according to God's good pleasure and the needs of their generations.

These special vocations in no way diminish the more general call to Christians to be Christ's ambassadors for peace and his partners in peacemaking. We are invited to pray for peace and to work for peace. All that we have to do is to offer ourselves for this work of prayer for the sake of the Kingdom and leave the outcome to God.

Whenever I get downhearted about praying for peace, I remember one of the stories in Pax Christi's first volume of peace sayings and stories for each day of the year:

'Tell me the weight of a snowflake,' a coal-mouse asked a wild dove.

'Nothing more than nothing,' was the answer.

'In that case I must tell you a marvellous story,' said the coal-mouse.

'I sat on the branch of a fir, close to its trunk, when it began to snow, not heavily, not a giant blizzard, no, just like in a dream, without any violence. Since I didn't have anything better to do, I counted the snowflakes settling on the twigs and needles of my branch.

'Their number was exactly 3,741,952. When the next snowflake dropped on the branch – nothing more than nothing, as you say – the branch broke off.'

Having said that, the coal-mouse flew away.

The dove, since Noah's time an authority on the matter, thought about the story for a while and finally said to herself: 'Perhaps there is only one person's voice lacking for peace to come about in the world.'[18]

'If it's not my voice that's going to bring the peace,' I think, 'then maybe I'm one of the three million or so voices that have to speak before the last one is heard.' Who knows? It helps anyway.

CHAPTER 11

COMPANIONSHIP IN THE TASK

༄

May he save your foot from stumbling (Ps. 121: 3)

*Christian prayer does not station the angel of the dew
in the midst of the fire, nor block the mouths of lions,
nor transfer to the hungry the peasant's dinner. It has
no special grace to avert the experience of suffering, but
it arms with endurance those who do suffer, who grieve,
who are pained. It makes grace multiply in power, so
that the faith may know what it obtains from the Lord,
while it understands what for God's name's sake it is
suffering.* (Tertullian, *On Prayer*)

IN 1944, when I was an undergraduate at Cambridge, I
came across a small grey-coloured booklet in a second-hand
bookshop. It was *Creative Suffering*, by the Russian writer Iulia
de Beausobre.[1] Opening the book at random, I found these
words:

In all ordinary circumstances a man must participate in
the deed done, if he is to participate in its redemption.
You can, of course, participate in such an evil deed either
as agent or patient, as causing or enduring the suffering
that marks it. And so intimately are good and evil intertwined that it is possible to gain your insight into God's
composition for the deed from either side.[2]

Those words arrested my attention. I did not understand them
but I sensed there was something there that spoke to my condition. I bought the book for one shilling and took it back to
college where I devoured the rest of it. I cannot say I grasped
much of what I read, but I was challenged by it.

I kept thinking about those words. At the time, I remember,

I was not wanting to participate in what I then thought of as 'the world and its evil deeds' at all. I wanted to 'dwell in the house of the Lord, all the days of my life, to behold the fair beauty of the Lord, and to seek him in his temple' (Ps. 23: 6, BCP 1666). I certainly didn't think of that kind of a life as a way of participating 'in the world', or in evil deeds. I was wrong, of course, but then I was young!

A year later I read de Beausobre's newly published novel on the life of St Seraphim, the eighteenth-century Russian Ortho-dox staretz and saint,[3] and found my life turned upside down by it. It gave me a glimpse of what a life of prayer was all about. Seraphim had spent many years of his life as a hermit deep in the forest of Temniki, isolated from all companionship save that of the forest creatures. Yet, as de Beausobre showed, he was intensely aware of everything that was going on in the world outside: through prayer he participated in the deeds done; through prayer and creative suffering he shared in Christ's redemptive work for the world. After many years of living the solitary life, Seraphim was called to become available to others, and he spent the last few years of his life outside the strict enclosure of the forest, and his monastery, as a staretz, a teacher, a healer, a man of prayer and wise counsel.

De Beausobre's message was clear. Through reading these two books I began to learn that you could 'participate in the deed done' either by physically being a part of it, or by sharing it through prayer. It is, of course, possible to do both. I still have both Iulia's books and I reread them at regular intervals. Their message has spoken to me in different ways at different times in my life. Since reading them I have read other books that have influenced the way I pray and live, and I have gained in personal experience, but these two books are still important to me.

In writing those words about participation 'in the deed done', if one is to 'participate in its redemption', Iulia was speaking from personal experience. After her marriage to Niko-lay de Beausobre in 1917 she and her husband had been sent to England by the Kerensky Provisional Government. They were there when the Tsarist regime was brought to an end. They decided to return and set off for Russia in January 1918.

Due to illness which held them up they did not reach their destination until a year later. Their arrival coincided with the birth of their son Dimitri.

They found a country in chaos: the Tsar and his family had been assassinated, civil war was still raging, people were hungry to the point of famine. The de Beausobre family members were no exception: they too went hungry. Iulia could not feed her son and although the couple bartered their possessions and clothes for milk he died from lack of nourishment at the age of four months. Stricken by grief, bowed down by the sufferings of extreme poverty, they left Russia and reached London, where Nikolay undertook work for the Soviet regime. But he ached to be back in Russia and in 1923 he returned. Iulia followed a year later.

They lived in Moscow and both worked for the State, but as a returned exile Nikolay came under suspicion. He spent several spells in prison on unspecified charges and one long period in exile, before being arrested for the last time on 5 February 1932 on a charge of plotting counter-revolutionary high treason. Six days later Iulia was arrested as a co-conspirator and taken to Lubyanka prison. There she suffered the mental torment of repeated interrogations at the hands of bullies who alternated cruelty with solicitude.

Although she was never physically tortured she was terrorised into agonising fear. One day, warned that she was to be taken to the examining officer, she felt so desperate with fear that she turned to Christ as her only hope. Before the jailer returned she had heard some words in the depths of her being: 'Peace. My peace be with you.' And as she was being taken out of her prison cell for the interrogation she heard some other words:

> Let peace stream to the left of you. Let peace stream to
> the right of you. Let peace remain awhile wherever you
> may tread. May it spread even to the furthest boundaries
> of the universe.[4]

Utterly calm she went to her tormentor. In prayer she had found her refuge in Christ. Eventually the interrogations stopped, her solitary confinement was ended and she was able to team up

with, and gain strength from being with, other political pris-
oners some of whom were devout Christians. With them she
learnt to suffer for Christ and to pray constantly.

Iulia had expected to be executed, but in 1933 she was sent
instead to a penal lumber camp in the Forest of Temniki near
the monastery where St Seraphim of Sarov had lived. There in
that penal camp, racked by repeated illnesses, she continued to
pray constantly. At the same time she did what work she could,
but she was too weak to be effective; after a few months, by
some mysterious reasoning of their own, the authorities decided
to release her.

Her freedom brought her the great sorrow of learning that
Nikolay had been shot nine months before on the 9 January
1933. She stayed in Russia for a while, living in conditions of
great hardship, but by great good fortune some of her English
friends decided to 'ransom' her by paying the Soviet government sufficient money to pay for her to go into exile. Iulia
arrived at the home of Isobel Paxton, who had once been her
governess in St Petersburg, in the spring of 1934.

Freedom inspired her to write about her sufferings, first in
a book about her imprisonment, *The Woman Who Could not
Die*,[5] then in the two books that I read a few years later. In her
writings it is clear that she participated in the evil 'deed done'
from the side of the suffering victim. Nevertheless, she shows
a deep understanding of the way in which some people can
participate from within evil. These people stand within the evil
in prayer, that is to say they feel they *are* evil, and are being
consumed, for instance, by hatred, blasphemy, murderous
impulses and perversions of all kinds. In extreme cases they
may commit evil acts. Yet, in some mysterious way, they give
all these evils to Christ so that they may be burnt up in the
flame of Love, the Blessed Trinity. The Russian 'yurodovy',
the 'fool for Christ's sake', is an example of this kind of 'participation from within evil' and is well understood by those steeped
in the Orthodox tradition as Iulia was.[6]

Her subsequent life in exile was made happy by her second
marriage.[7] She remained a firm believer, a member of the
Russian Orthodox Church and a considerable influence in
many people's lives, including my own. I met her only on two

occasions – both so memorable – just three years before her death on 20 December 1977.

Iulia was one of those people who are transparent: in them we see the human face of the Holy Spirit.[8] In them we can find peace made manifest. Through her peace did indeed 'spread to the boundaries of the universe', or so it seemed to me when I met her for the first time and asked what she was doing. 'Scouring the face of the earth,' she replied, 'using the carnal remnants of my decomposing body as a rag in God's hands to cleanse the world of its many pollutions.'[9] I could not fathom how this could happen, but all the same I could, and can, appreciate that the prayers of God's children can have a counter-acting and neutralising effect on evil. I suspect that is as close to understanding her perplexing statement as I can come at present.

The words Iulia spoke to me at the end of her life are linked to the words she wrote when she first came to England. I was struck then, and still am, by her insistence that 'in all ordinary circumstances, a man must participate in the deed done if he is to participate in its redemption'. I think that in our own time God is calling Christians to participate fully in the world as it is, in all its sin and ugliness, as well as in all its beauty and goodness, and through prayer to participate in its redemption.

As I have already said in the Introduction to this book, this vocation is ordinary, not extraordinary or even unusual. It is, in one sense, what all baptised Christians do. It seems to me, however, that some of us who live 'in the world' can sometimes be somewhat disparaging about ourselves. Just as one can some-times hear women saying, somewhat apologetically, 'I'm *just* a housewife,' one can hear people saying, 'I'm nothing special, *just* an ordinary Christian.' We are all special to God; we are all part of the Body of Christ; we are all called to share in his redemptive work; we are all called to glory. Within the Body some of us are asked to make prayer our main focus.

Prayer as a way of life that is part of Christ's redemptive work in the face of evil is a glorious vocation. It is not a second best to any other form of baptismal life, neither is it better than any other way of discipleship. It is just one way of following Jesus. It is the way by which those who are called to it become most fully human, most fully the people God meant them to become.

Anyone, anyone at all, can hear this call to a life of prayer and resistance to evil. Nevertheless, there are some family likenesses about those who are called to focus their lives on the prayer that also involves resistance to evil. They are usually men and women of a contemplative disposition: that is to say they have an inbuilt tendency to look for meaning below the surface appearance of created things, creatures, people and events. They esteem 'being' as well as 'doing', so they often value themselves and other people for who they are, rather than for what they do. They are often 'broken' people who have plumbed the depths of personal suffering, but who are humble enough to limp along and ask for help on the journey. They are generous people who want to offer themselves to God for whatever work God wants them to do. They seldom fit easily into a mould. Quite often they are stubborn people. They have to be if they are to stand their ground against the evils God wants them to oppose.

What has struck me quite forcibly in recent years is that we all need help if we are to do our work for Christ. Christians are now a minority in Western society. Evil is rampant. If we are to make a concerted effort to give ourselves to God in prayer, if we are to resist evil and to stand our ground, we need each other's encouragement, support and help. Otherwise it is easy to get swamped by the evils we are trying to resist, whatever they are and however strong we feel we are.

I have been looking to see what help is available from the established Christian communities. The answers are interesting. The evangelical and Pentecostal Churches lay great emphasis on personal prayer. They have strong ministries of intercession, healing and deliverance which can help men and women who find themselves in an awkward place in the cosmic struggle against evil. Charismatic movements within all denominational Churches have their dangers, but their emphasis on the power and gifts of the Holy Spirit is helpful to many people.

Catholic and Orthodox Churches, using those terms in their broadest sense, stress the importance of the sacraments of baptism and Holy Communion in the struggle against personal sin

and corporate and cosmic evil. These have great healing power
in people's lives. The sacraments of reconciliation and anointing
with oil for healing are also helpful to many people.

It seems to me that those of us who take prayer and resistance
to evil seriously need to make use of whatever help we can get
from our own tradition. Nevertheless I have discovered many
Christians in all denominations who find themselves left out
on a limb. They do not seem to find it easy to get the help
they need wholly from within their own tradition. Two strongly
evangelical Christians, for instance, have recently told me that
they feel that they need Holy Communion more often than is
usual in their own Churches. A charismatic Christian told me
that she longed for more silence in her services. Several Christians whose prayer takes the form of a quiet looking at God
have recently asked for help because they are so full of love
that they want to burst out with it. They would do so were it
not for the fact that overt expressions of joy seem unacceptable
within their own Church congregations.

Christians whose prayer takes the form of a quiet gazing at
God, or a beating upon the cloud of unknowing, seem to
find it particularly difficult to get the kind of help they need.
Sometimes this may be because they are too shy or proud to
ask for help and so they try to 'go it alone'. More often, I
think, it is because there is in all denominations a dearth of
parish-based clergy who have experience of the more seamy
sides of the battle against evil in prayer. It is true that there is
a wonderful heritage in the writings of some of the great people
of prayer who have been God's servants in former generations.
Such writings contain eternal truths, but they also contain
insights that were appropriate to their own times and settings
but are less helpful to our own generation. The best of these
writings can, however, transcend cultural differences.

Those who are drawn to the prayer of emptiness and quiet
gazing are, it seems to me, particularly vulnerable to temptation
in prayer. If resistance to evil becomes part of our life of prayer,
we are likely to find ourselves standing at first on the sidelines
of the battlefield between good and evil. After a time we are
likely to become part of the battlefield. Still later, we may find
that we have become part of the battle, participating in the

redemptive work of Christ either from within our identification with good, or from the opposite pole of evil, as the 'yurodovy' does, or from both points of view at one and the same time.

My personal experience of prayer, both my own and other people's, suggests that Christians can 'go it alone' quite easily up to a certain point. So long as they remain on the sidelines of the battlefield over which the cosmic struggle between good and evil is taking place, it will be all right to assume sole responsibility for their lives of prayer. Once they become the place where this cosmic encounter is happening, they will be aware of the conflict that is going on, although they are not directly involved in the struggle. Such people are in greater need of help than they were when they were spectators: they can benefit from a good soul friend and membership of a supportive group of people who take prayer seriously. However, as soon as they become participants in the battle itself they cannot, in my opinion, expect to survive temptation unless they have both guidance and companionship. This is because in that kind of prayer angels of darkness are so good at seeming like angels of light that the temptation to go down the wrong track is both subtle and highly dangerous. The road to hell is, indeed, 'paved with good intentions'.[10] I have personally known several men and women of impeccable faith seduced into evil actions by thinking that they were doing good ones.

It can be a frightening experience to find yourself cast as a battlefield or even an active participant in the cosmic struggle between good and evil. So I think that Christians called to this work need all the help they can get, and in order to get it they are likely to need to cross the boundaries of their own traditions within the Church to find that help.

Some Christians do find that their parish provides them with all the support they need, but many turn to religious communities for help, others to Julian groups,[11] meditation groups or prayer workshops.

Christians who want to develop good rhythms of prayer so that they can 'pray constantly' can benefit greatly from developing a close association with an established religious community. Religious communities are well accustomed to providing support for their close friends and associates. Many allow lay people to become oblates, tertiaries and associates: that kind of membership brings with it a very real sense of mutual companionship and this is very valuable to people living lives of prayer outside monastic communities. There are a few religious communities that allow their very closest adherents to share fully in the life of the community when those who live in the world come to stay at the monastery.[12]

As yet, there seem to be only a few religious communities that can envisage some of their members living outside the community while others live together as a core group. Certainly the Grail, a Roman Catholic secular institute,[13] has core group members who live together as well as outside members who return to the main house for at least two weeks in each year. However within some Roman Catholic communities there are a growing number of 'religious' living alone outside their communities. The religious communities and secular institutes that permit this kind of arrangement are not, however, contemplative monastic communities. I do know of one Roman Catholic monastery and a number of Anglican monasteries that permit life-professed members to live as hermits away from the community,[14] but to my knowledge there are no contemplative religious orders that permit people to train with them with a view to their eventually living wholly outside the community except for periods of return for rest, refreshment and renewal.

There seems to be a fear that such a policy would weaken the core group and stop people from testing their vocations to contemplative monasticism. This, to my mind, is a pity. Those who live in community according to established patterns of traditional monasticism and those who live in less traditional, newer forms of contemplative religious life have a great deal in common, although the expressions of their vocations take different forms. I think there are strong reasons for the closest possible association between the established religious orders and these newer forms of monasticism. Both would benefit from the cross-fertilisation that mutual goals, training and close association could provide.

I realise that there would be plenty of dangers if such a policy were ever to be implemented. Those dangers would be very similar to the ones associated with training full-time stipendiary clergy alongside non-stipendiary clergy, some of whom will remain in secular employment. Their needs after ordination may, and often do, differ: class differentials may operate to the detriment of the non-stipendiary ministers; they may lose contact with each other. Nevertheless, my personal belief is that close associations between contemplative monastics living in core groups within monasteries and convents and those living alone, or in small groups, in ordinary houses would be beneficial to them and to the whole Church.

It is interesting to note that Dr Hilary Wakeman,[15] the founder of the Julian groups, was hoping to start a new kind of ecumenical religious order for lay contemplatives when she first started looking round for support for lay people who 'were trying to combine contemplative and secular lives'.[16] Instead, she found a large number of people who did not want to belong to any order, or have a Rule of Life, but who did want to meet regularly and to pray together in a contemplative way. A number of groups were formed and they have steadily grown. Now this movement is international. As Dr Wakeman says:

> there are only three criteria for Julian groups – that they be Christ centred, based on contemplative prayer and at least potentially multi-denominational – they could in theory be very different from each other. No laws are laid down as to the structure of meetings: groups are encouraged to find out what is right for *them*. Yet most of them eventually move into a common pattern of starting with a brief reading, having half an hour's silence and ending with a prayer said together.[17]

If one finds a religious community, Julian group or other contemplative prayer group to join, it seems to be important that the belonging is real enough for all to be able to share their difficulties in prayer. Otherwise members lose their sense of mutuality and interdependence that is so vital to finding a balance between togetherness and solitude.

An interesting contemporary development that has come to my attention has been the increase in the number of people joining contemplative prayer groups and/or base communities. In Britain and the United States of America many of these base communities have originated in the Roman Catholic communities. Some are ecumenical. Ten or twelve people commonly join together in a locality to pray together, eat bread together and take action by consensus. One explanation for the rise in base communities in Western society may be that Church congregations are too large to provide the warm sense of belonging that most of us need if we are to live out our faith with integrity. Smaller groups can help a great deal provided they do not become cliques, divorced from the active worship and life of their local Church.

There are, however, many people who are not catered for because their needs do not quite match with what is already on offer. They are contemplative *and* active. They hide in God, yet are impelled by the Spirit to witness in the world. They are retiring, yet zealous in intercession: this is their share in the apostolic mission of the whole Church. A few pray during the night, yet have to follow their Lord into the city by day. Some of these Christians are strong enough to walk alone. Others, like myself, are quite solitary in disposition yet know their need of companionship along the way.

There are a few groups that seek to provide support for such people. One such group is the Fellowship of Solitaries.[18] This was started by Peter Edwards in 1984. Members receive a quarterly newsletter that focuses on contemplative prayer and the solitary way. The Fellowship is ecumenical. Its members know that one can have a solitary disposition and a call to solitary prayer and sometimes to periods of solitude without necessarily having to live alone, so the Fellowship includes married people as well as people who live on their own. The group is self-selecting. There are no rules and no organised meetings, though a membership address list is available and so there are opportunities for meeting if people want to do so.

I have personally learnt a great deal from a small ecumenical network of Christians who call themselves the Companions of Jesus Crucified.[19] In this network there are no limiting boundaries or hard and fast rules, and yet each member is committed to prayer as a way of life. There are as many ways of living a life of prayer in the world as there are people. Circumstances differ so widely that having defined corporate rules and regulations might exclude the very people who most needed the support of the network. Paradoxically we are finding community within this loose bonding of a network.

When we began I wrote a gentle set of guidelines to help members to find personal rhythms that would help them to live lives of prayer and resistance to some of the evils that I have described.[20] Within these guidelines each of us develops a pattern that is helpful. Some people thrive on spontaneity. Others choose to keep a simple rule because it is helpful to them. Each person does this in his or her own way, and each is encouraged to have the help of a soul friend or spiritual director as well as belonging to the network.

We offer support to one another as each of us tries to live a life of prayer in the world. Each of us has a unique God-given identity and purpose in life and we live our discipleship individually, but we do have a common focus in that we are gathered around the person of Jesus on the cross. In us, individually and corporately, you can find all the characters who were present at the crucifixion. As we have learnt more about what it means to be a Companion, most of us can find all those characters, good and bad, in our own personalities. We differ from the Fellowship of Solitaries, to which some of us also belong, in that each of us knows, or is willing to get to know, at least one other person in the network personally: often we know several people. Although we seldom meet as an entire group, we do try to maintain personal contact through local meetings and through a newsletter. Some of us are able to visit each other's homes. In one area, where several of us live, between two and six people meet regularly for silent prayer. Several of us have met twice for an annual retreat/conference, and we hope to go on doing so. These personal friendships and contacts help us to grow closer to each other. Gradually, as we have come to understand more about each other's individual vocations, we have also come to feel close to each other, able to write or telephone for moral and spiritual support when we need it.

There is no hierarchy in the network and very little in the way of organisation. The only sign of our commitment is that we each have a simple wooden cross, which some of us wear openly and others do not. The original ten were hand-carved out of the same piece of wood. Each is alike, yet each is unique.

This small gathering of people around the cross is only one tiny part of a greater body of people who pray constantly and try to witness to the primacy of Christ in their lives. There are doubtless many other ways of providing the kind of companionship that is both supportive and nourishing. Christians who feel a need for such a group should not hesitate to try to find one. If none exists nearby, it is good to start a local one.

In today's world there is an urgent need for Christians to resist the evils of our own generation. We shall never do that by paying attention to the evil, protesting about it, combatting it by lament for the old days, inveighing against those who live egocentric lives. We shall only accomplish our task of witness for Christ by following him. It will be through living fulfilled and joyful lives that we shall proclaim our belief in Christ's victory over evil. That victory has to be proclaimed anew in every generation according to its circumstances.

In the preceding chapters of this book I have suggested some areas of social life in late twentieth-century Western society where I think there is need for Christians to live differently from many of their fellow citizens. If any of us are to 'stand up' to the devil, 'strong in faith and in the knowledge that it is the same kind of suffering that the community of your brothers (and sisters) throughout the world is undergoing' (1 Pet. 5: 9), then we will rely on each other's example and prayerful support for our encouragement (1 Thess. 5: 10–11).

All Christians are called 'to turn to Christ, repent of our sins and renounce evil'.[21] Those who have dedicated their lives to the service of God through prayer can help all of us to find our own place in God's work for our own generation. All that matters is that we should find our own way of expressing our own particular Christian calling through the way we live our lives alone and in relation to others. We will benefit from the kind of support that St Paul gave to the Christians at Ephesus. His voice still speaks insistently to us across the two thousand years that separate us in time but unite us in eternity:

Finally, grow strong in the Lord, with the strength of his

power. Put on the full armour of God so as to be able to resist the devil's tactics. For it is not against human enemies that we have to struggle, but against the principalities and the ruling forces who are masters of the darkness in this world, the spirits of evil in the heavens. That is why you must take up all God's armour, or you will not be able to put up any resistance on the evil day, or stand your ground even though you exert yourselves to the full.

So stand your ground, with truth as a belt round your waist, and uprightness a breastplate, wearing for shoes on your feet the eagerness to spread the gospel of peace and always carrying the shield of faith so that you can use it to quench the burning arrows of the evil one. And then you must take salvation as your helmet and the sword of the Spirit, that is, the word of God.

In all your prayer and entreaty keep praying in the Spirit on every possible occasion. Never get tired of staying awake to pray for all God's holy people, and pray for me to be given opportunity to open my mouth and fearlessly make known the mystery of the Gospel of which I am an ambassador in chains; pray that in proclaiming it I may speak as fearlessly as I ought to do. (Eph. 6: 10–20)

As baptised Christians, whether we be in fetters for the sake of Christ, or bound to Christ by bonds of love, we are set free from enslavement to evil and sin and we are called to be ambassadors to our present generation. This text is our text. May it serve to unite and support us in our discipleship, as we work in our varied ways for the coming of God's Kingdom on earth.

NOTES

❦

Introduction. Pray and Stand Firm

1. Basil Hume, *To Be a Pilgrim* (St Paul, 1984), p. 137.
2. To contemplate God is to look at God. In this context I am using the phrase to describe the kind of prayer where one focuses one's whole attention on God rather than meditating discursively about God.
3. By a contemplative dispostion I mean an ability to look below the surface of the object or person one is looking at to see the deeper meaning or implications.
4. These words are taken from the Preface to the Thanksgiving Prayer in the Book of Common Prayer, 1666.
5. This is a term used to describe groups of people who gather for discernment of their basic needs, mutual encouragement and upbuilding of morale so that positive action to secure their rights can be taken by the whole group. It was first used in Latin America, where very poor people formed communities to fight for human rights. Base communities are now being established in Western societies.
6. See Geoffrey Curtis CR, *William of Glasshampton* (SPCK, 1947; 2nd edn 1978); Brother Ramon SSF, *A Hidden Fire* (SPCK, 1978; Marshall Pickering, 1985); Alan Whittemore OHC, *Joy in Holiness* (New York, Holy Cross Press, 1964).
7. A hermit is someone who lives in solitude, not necessarily always in the same place.
8. An anchorite or anchoress is a hermit who is rooted in one spot, usually very close to a church.
9. A lay contemplative lives a life of solitary prayer in the world, not necessarily alone.
10. 'Kingdom values' is a term that describes a set of values directly derived from Jesus' teaching about the Kingdom of heaven. These values can be found in the Sermon on the Mount and in the parables and teachings of Jesus elsewhere in the New Testament.
11. St Augustine, *Confessions*, tr. and ed. Owen Chadwick (Cambridge University Press, 1991), book 1, p. 3.
12. See Vladimir Lossky, *Mystical Theology of the Eastern Church* (James Clarke & Son, 1957), pp, 196ff.
13. See *The Cloud of Unknowing*, ed. Clifton Wolters (Penguin Books, 1961).

14. An Orthodox form of prayer which is rhythmically repeated over and over again. The full form is 'Lord Jesus Christ, Son of the Living God, have mercy on me, a sinner', but it is often shortened to the use of the Holy Name of Jesus, said in time to the rhythm of one's breathing.
15. For further help on mystical experience see William James, *The Varieties of Religious Experience* (Longman Green, 1902).
16. See Owen Chadwick, *Cassian*, 2nd edn (Cambridge University Press, 1968); Dermott Chitty, *The Desert a City* (Oxford University Press, 1966); Peter Anson, *The Call of the Desert* (SPCK, 1964).
17. This is a reference to the controversies about the beliefs of Don Cupitt and his followers.
18. The Little Brothers and Sisters of Jesus are a prime example of a modern religious community who find their desert in cities. The Jerusalem Community is another community that devotes itself to contemplative prayer at the heart of the city.
19. Companions of Jesus Crucified. See Chapter 11.

Chapter 1. Pray and Stand Firm

1. I have seen this in a life of John Wesley and have heard about it from Methodists whom I know, but I have not been able to find the direct reference.
2. These alternative ideas must also be consistent with reason and the developing tradition of the Church to which they belong.
3. In reading the Bible it is right to consider the work of many biblical scholars, who point out ways in which the texts were written and edited. Study is enjoyable, but in the end it is the words that reverberate in many people's minds, including my own. Those words are interpreted to us by the Spirit, at particular times of our lives; they influence our attitudes and govern our behaviour. I therefore make no apology for my reflective approach to scripture, even though it might seem too literal for some people.

Chapter 2. Prayer for Busy People

1. Divine Office, book II, p. 21.
2. The Bible Reading Fellowship provides a series of different commentaries every year that can be helpful. Personally I find that *The Interpreter's Bible*, ed. Buttrick et al. (New York/Nashville, Abingdon-Cokesbury Press, 1952), and any of William Barclay's commentaries are the most helpful way of deepening my understanding of God's word.

3. See *The Way of a Pilgrim* (anon.), tr. R. M. French (Philip Allan, 1930) and Per-Olof Sjörgen, *The Jesus Prayer*, tr. Sidney Linton (SPCK, 1975).

4. Thomas Merton, *Conjectures of a Guilty Bystander*, 2nd edn (Sheldon Press, 1977), pp. 153–4.

5. *Revelations of Divine Love*, Julian of Norwich, tr. and ed. Clifton Wolters (Penguin Books, 1966).

6. Elie Wiesel, *Night* (Robson Books, London, 1974; Penguin Books, 1981, pp. 75ff.)

7. There were many broadcasts about this issue in January/February 1995, and this account is based on one of them.

8. Gerard Manley Hopkins, 'Wreck of the Deutschland'.

9. This idea is expanded on in Chapters 10 and 11.

Chapter 3. Seeking the Treasure

1. Henry James, 'The Figure in the Carpet', *Collected Volumes of Short Stories*, vol. 10 (London, Rupert Hart Davis, 1896).

2. See note 10 to the Introduction.

3. See Dorothy Day, *The Long Loneliness* (Harper & Row, 1952) and Jim Forest, *Love is the Measure*, a biography of Dorothy Day (Marshall Pickering, 1986).

4. See Charles Elliott, *Praying the Kingdom, Towards a Political Spirituality* (Darton, Longman & Todd, 1985).

5. Ibid. p. 6.

6. Richard Foster, *Money, Sex and Power* (Hodder & Stoughton, 1985).

7. See *Praying the Kingdom* pp. 22–33, and *Money, Sex and Power*, pp. 59–60.

8. *Praying the Kingdom*, p. 31.

9. Isaac Bashevis Singer, *Stories for Children* (New York, Farrar, Strauss & Giroux, 1962).

10. Ibid, p. 253.

Chapter 4. The Joy of Belonging

1. J. B. Priestley, *An Inspector Calls* (Heinemann, 1947), Act III, p. 57.

2. L'Arche was started by Jean Vanier in 1964. His book *Community and Growth* (Darton, Longman & Todd, 1979) is informative about new styles of community life.

3. See *The Shorter Oxford English Dictionary*, 3rd edn (Oxford, Oxford University Press, 1947), p. 993, and *The Reader's Digest Universal Dictionary* (Reader's Digest, 1987), p. 785.

4. John Donne, *Devotions*.

5. St Teresa of Avila, *The Life of St Teresa*, tr. J. M. Cohen, ed. E. V. Rien (Penguin Books 1957).
6. The Vicarage, Tamworth in Arden, Solihull, West Midlands, B94 5EB.
7. 80 Herbert Road, Rainham, Gillingham, ME8 9HP.
8. Dietrich Bonhoeffer, *Life Together* (SCM Press, 1955), p. 67.
9. I have heard this phrase from several vicars and Church leaders.
10. L'Arche, 14 London Road, Beccles, Suffolk, NR34 9NH.
11. St Francis House, Normanby Road, Scunthorpe, South Humberside, DN15 6AR.
12. Focalare, 3 Abbeville Road, London SW4 9LA or 34 Earl's Court Square, London SW5.

Chapter 5. Finding Our Humanity

1. Franz Pfeiffer, *Meister Eckhardt*, tr. C. de B. Evans (John M. Watkins, 1956), vol. 1, p. 436.
2. Jean Vanier, founder of L'Arche.
3. William Law, *The Spirit of Love*, ed. Sidney Spencer (James Clarke, 1968), p. 207.
4. This is the doctrine of realised eschatology. I find these words from Archbishop Michael Ramsey's writings helpful: 'Heaven is the goal of man, and heaven gives the true perspective for our present life. Our belief in the goal of heaven goes with our belief in the infinite and eternal worth of every man, woman and child created in God's own image and reminds us that we are called to nothing less than Christ-like perfection of the saints.' Michael Ramsey, *Through the Year with Michael Ramsey*, ed. Margaret Duggan (Hodder & Stoughton, 1975), p. 253.
5. Iona Community, Iona, Mull, Scotland.
6. Told by Revd Mother Gillian Mary to the community at Tymawr and also two years later by Father Victor de Waal, Chaplain to the community. A more elaborate version is to be found in M. Scott Peck, *The Different Drum* (Arrow, 1990), pp. 13–15.

Chapter 6. Sacred Idleness

1. George MacDonald, *Wilfred Cumbermede* (Hurst & Blackett, 1972), vol. III, p. 169.
2. Found in *A Treasury of Quotations on Christian Themes*, ed. Carroll E. Simcox (SPCK, 1976), no. 2689.
3. Luke 2: 49. A man like Andrew would, of course, only use the King James (Authorised Version) Bible.
4. Gen. 2: 24 (AV).
5. The full text of the Latin tag is *Orare est laborare, laborare est orare*.

See *The Oxford Dictionary of Qutations*, 2nd edn (London, Oxford University Press, 1953), p. 13.
6. Rule of St Benedict, Chapter 48.
7. *A Treasury of Quotations on Christian Themes*, ed. Carroll E. Simcox (SPCK, 1976), no. 2678.
8. See Una Kroll, *TMA Signpost for the World* (Darton, Longman & Todd, 1974), Chapter 3, pp. 53–67 for a discussion of the effects of transcendental meditation on alpha waves in EEGs.
9. Skilled teachers are needed to teach one of these techniques. Local centres are usually advertised. In the case of transcendental meditation there is usually a fee involved. Some Christians do not like adopting methods that come from traditions other than their own.
10. This refers to the charismatic gift of letting oneself be influenced so completely by the Holy Spirit that one dances in a kind of ecstasy. It is a very gentle and beautiful gift.
11. A Chinese martial art 'consisting in a series of movements, performed slowly and deliberately, for training both the body and the mind in balance, control and co-ordinaton' (*The Reader's Digest Universal Dictionary*, p. 1540).
12. This form of dance tunes in to the earth's rhythms. It is often very healing.

Chapter 7. The Delight of Reverence

1. William Sykes, *Visions of Love* (Oxford, Bible Reading Fellowship, 1992), p. 211.
2. This comes from my experience of working in a psychiatric hospital on the outskirts of London in the 1970s, when I encountered two patients who had been on LSD as a 'short cut'. Each had a bad 'trip' and one went on to develop schizophrenia.
3. Brother Lawrence, *The Practice of the Presence of God*, tr. Donald Attwater (London/Tunbridge Wells, Burns & Oates, 1977).
4. The spiritual equivalents of 'short cuts' come through hallucinogenic drugs, prolonged fasting, self-induced trances and ecstatic dancing akin to that practised by the dervishes.
5. Anthony Bloom, *School for Prayer* (Darton, Longman & Todd, 1970), pp. 60–1.
6. Little Sisters of the Poor, St Peter's, Meadow Road, London SW5 1QH.

Chapter 8. The Music of Silence

1. For example, Moses on the mountain-top, Joseph in prison, Isaiah smitten by his vision, Jeremiah down a pit.
2. Lucia Santos was one of those illiterate children who saw a vision of a lady at Fatima on 13 May 1917 and on five other occasions. She became a Carmelite nun.
3. An ancient Hindu technique for meditation, revived and brought to the West by Maharishi Mahesh Yogi in 1964. It is individually taught by those who have themselves learnt the technique. It is widely available in Western society.
4. Dag Hammarskjöld, *Markings*, tr. W. H. Auden and Leif Sjöberg (London, Faber & Faber, 1964), p. 85.
5. Found in *Peacemaking Day by Day*, vol. 1 (Pax Christi, 1989).

Chapter 9. Loving God's Creation

1. Fyodor Dostoyevsky, *The Brothers Karamazov*, tr. David Magarshack (Penguin Books, 1958), p. 375.
2. See the first five books of the Bible, the psalms and the book of Sirach for references to the grandeur of God's creation, the majesty of God's power over nature and the terrifying aspects of God's sovereignty.
3. This happened to me. I killed the mamba.
4. Fyodor Dostoyevsky, *The Brothers Karamazov*, tr. David Magarshack (Penguin Books, 1958), p. 375.
5. For the full text see Nicholas de Cusa, *The Vision of God*, tr. Emily Gurney Salter (Frederick Ungar, 1928), pp. 61–2.
6. Teilhard de Chardin, *Hymn of the Universe* (Collins Fount, 1970), p. 30.
7. John Polkinghorne, *One World* (SPCK, 1986), pp. 97–8.
8. Alan Ereira, *The Heart of the World* (Jonathan Cape, 1992), p. 10.
9. Life Style, c/o Denise Moll, 21 Fleetwood Court, Madeira Road, West Byfleet, Surrey, KT4 6VE.

Chapter 10. Making Peace

1. Thomas à Kempis, *The Imitation of Christ*, ed. Ludwig Curtis, tr. Ludwig Weiland (Routledge and Kegan Paul, 1949), p. 295.
2. This refers to the killing of James Bolger in 1993.
3. This refers to the killing of Mrs Phyllis Saville on her way to church in March 1994.
4. René Girard, *Violence and the Sacred* (Johns Hopkins University Press, 1977); Raymund Schwager SJ, *Must There be Scapegoats?*

Violence and Redemption in the Bible (Harper & Row, 1987); James Alison OP, *Knowing Jesus* (SPCK, 1993).

5. Paul Tournier, *The Violence Inside* (SCM, 1978), p. 66.
6. Ibid. p. 67.
7. Iulia de Beausobre, *Flame in the Snow* (Constable, 1945).
8. Ibid, p. 95.
9. Ibid, p. 111.
10. Ibid, pp. 147–8.
11. Thomas à Kempis, *The Imitation of Christ*.
12. Valentine Zander, *St Seraphim of Sarov*, tr. Sister Gabriel Anne SSC (London, SPCK, 1975), p. x.
13. Satish Kumar, *Prayers for Peace* 70 (Weymouth Road, Frome, Somerset, BA1 1HY).
14. Little has been written about this subject, but the best dispassionate account I know is to be found in Iulia de Beausobre's pamphlet *Creative Suffering* (Dacre Press, 1940), pp. 37–45.
15. H. M. Prestcott, *The Man on a Donkey*, vol. 2 (Eyre & Spottiswode, 1952).
16. Ibid, p. 688.
17. Ibid, p. 682.
18. Kurt Kauter, 'New Fables Thus Spoken – "The Carabon" ', in *Peacemaking Day by Day*, vol. 1 (Pax Christi, 1989), p. 52.

Chapter 11. Companionship in the Task

1. Iulia de Beausobre, *Creative Suffering* (Dacre Press, 1940).
2. Ibid, p. 41.
3. Iulia de Beausobre, *Flame in the Snow* (Constable, 1945).
4. Constance Babington-Smith, *Iulia de Beausobre* (Darton, Longman & Todd, 1983), p. 31.
5. Iulia de Beausobre, *The Woman Who Could not Die* (Victor Gollancz, 1938).
6. See Iulia Beausobre, *Creative Suffering*, p. 45; John Saward, *Perfect Fools* (Oxford, Oxford University Press, 1980).
7. She became Lady Namier. She published her husband's biography, *Lewis Namier* (Oxford University Press, 1971).
8. See Vladimir Lossky, *The Mystical Theology of the Eastern Church* (James Clarke & Son, 1957).
9. Personal conversation, but a fuller explanation can be found in *Iulia de Beausobre*, pp. 112–16.
10. Ben Johnson. Quoted in *The Shorter Oxford English Dictionary* (Oxford, Oxford University Press, 1947), p. 1023, where the quotation reads 'Hell is paved with good intentions'. The misquotation seems to have entered common usage.

11. Details of Julian Meetings can be obtained from 80 Herbert Road, Rainham, Gillingham, Kent, ME8 9HP.
12. For example The Society of the Love of God, Fairacres, Oxford, an Anglican monastic community where the oblates wear a simple habit when they stay with the community and live in the same rhythm as the nuns.
13. The Grail, 125 Waxwell Lane, Pinner, Middlesex.
14. Stanbrook Abbey, Worcester; Society of the Love of God, Oxford; Community of the Holy Name, Derby; Society of the Sacred Cross, Monmouth.
15. Now an Anglican priest working in the Diocese of Norwich.
16. Hilary Wakeman, 'Beginnings', in Robert Llewellyn (ed.) *Circles of Silence* (Darton, Longman & Todd, 1994), p. 5.
17. Ibid, p. 7.
18. c/o Mrs Eve Baker, Coed Glas, Talgarth Road, Bronllys, Powys, LD3 0HN.
19. Contact person is Sister Una CJC, St Mary's Lodge, Priory Street, Monmouth, Gwent NP5 3BR.
20. Available from the above address.
21. Baptismal promise according to the Alternative Service Book of the Church of England.

SELECT BIBLIOGRAPHY

❦

Prayer

Hans Urs von Balthasar, *Prayer*, London, Geoffrey Chapman, 1963.

Igumen Chariton of Valamo, *The Art of Prayer, an Orthodox Anthology*, ed. K. T. Ware, tr. E. Kadlonbovsky and E. M. Palmer, London, Faber & Faber, 1966.

Thomas Merton, *Contemplative Prayer*, London, Darton, Longman & Todd, 1973.

Hubert Northcott, *The Venture of Prayer*, London, SPCK, 1950.

Prayer in Action

A. M. Allchin (ed.) *Solitude and Communion*, Oxford, SLG Press, 1983.

Gerald Arbuckle, *Refounding the Church*, London, Geoffrey Chapman, 1993.

Owen Chadwick, *John Cassian*, Cambridge, Cambridge University Press, 1968.

Charles Elliott, *Praying the Kingdom, Towards a Political Spirituality*, London, Darton, Longman & Todd, 1985.

Charles Elliott, *Praying through Paradox*, London, Collins Fount, 1987.

Richard Foster, *Celebration of Discipline*, London, Hodder & Stoughton, 1983.

Richard Foster, *Freedom of Simplicity*, London, Hodder & Stoughton, 1984.

Richard Foster, *Money, Sex and Power*, London, Hodder & Stoughton, 1985.

Donald Nicholl, *Holiness*, London, Darton, Longman & Todd, 1981.

Joan Puls, *Seek Treasures in Small Fields*, London, Darton, Longman & Todd, 1993.